PLANNING AND DRAFTING FOR THE GENERATION-SKIPPING TRANSFER TAX

Second Edition

American Law Institute American Bar Association Committee on Continuing Professional Education

ALI ABA

4025 Chestnut Street, Philadelphia, Pennsylvania 19104-3099

PLANNING AND DRAFTING FOR THE GENERATION-SKIPPING TRANSFER TAX

Second Edition

Jerold I. Horn
of the Illinois and
Pennsylvania Bars

ALI ABA
American Law Institute- American Bar Association
Committee on Continuing Professional Education
4025 Chestnut Street, Philadelphia, PA 19104-3099

Library of Congress Catalog Number: 93-074943

First Edition December 1990. Second Edition 1994

Printed in the United States of America

ISBN: 0-8318-0724-5

James D. Maugans of the ALI-ABA staff
supervised the production of this book

Earlier versions of parts of this work appeared in the UNIVERSITY OF SOUTHERN CALIFORNIA FORTIETH TAX INSTITUTE (1988), © 1988 by Matthew Bender & Company, Inc., Albany, New York; in 13 PROBATE NOTES No. 4 (Spring 1988) and in 14 PROBATE NOTES No. 3 (Winter 1988). PROBATE NOTES is a publication of the American College of Probate Counsel, now the American College of Trust and Estate Counsel.

To the memory
of the late
A. James Casner

Foreword

Among its efforts to close perceived loopholes in the existing fabric of the Internal Revenue Code via the Tax Reform Act of 1976, Congress created a new species of tax: the generation-skipping transfer tax on transfers in trust to each generation two or more below the transferor. The tax, as enacted in 1976, was widely perceived as unworkable, dooming its original incarnation.

The Tax Reform Act of 1986 repealed the tax and replaced it with a new version. Added to the estate and gift taxes on transfers of property, this third layer of taxation is designed to ensure that most transfers of property or interests therein — whether *inter vivos*, testamentary, or in trust — are subject to taxation at the level of each generation. Jerold I. Horn has been involved with the tax since its first development in 1976, and he has considered, argued, lectured, and written upon it for more than 17 years. In his opinion, the current version is probably here to stay, although the actual administration of the tax will determine its long-term prospects.

Planning and Drafting for the Generation-Skipping Transfer Tax is more than a mere analysis of the applicable statutes. Horn has taken the additional steps of addressing issues of strategy, preparing well-drafted documents that provide ample discretion and flexibility to those charged with their administration, and offering hypothetical drafting solutions for the varying situations practitioners face.

The first edition, published in December 1990, was supplemented in early 1993 to reflect changes resulting from the Proposed Temporary Regulations issued on December 24, 1992, and other adjustments by the author reflecting his current thinking about the allocation of property among shares set apart with respect to living and deceased children, in order to best use G8T exemption and the predeceased child exception. It also included new forms and refinements of forms that were in the first edition, based on the author's additional work with the tax. This second edition incorporates those changes and affords the author an opportunity to further refine the balance of the text.

ALI-ABA once again expresses its great appreciation to Jerold Horn for his willingness to share his expertise and experience with the bar through this book and his diligence in updating this material to offer readers the most current strategies for property distribution under the tax and its administrative regulations, as well as his generosity in contributing his time and efforts in furtherance of continuing legal education by participating in an assortment of ALI-ABA courses as a panel member.

SHARON T. WALSH
Director of Publications — Books
American Law Institute-
American Bar Association
Committee on Continuing
Professional Education

January 21, 1994

Preface

Congress enacted the gift tax as a "backstop" to the estate tax. The purpose was to reduce the use of lifetime transfers to avoid an excise tax upon transfers at death. Similarly, many years later, in 1976, Congress enacted the generation-skipping tax, as a backstop to both the gift tax and the estate tax. The purpose was to reduce the use of generation-skipping transfers to avoid an excise tax upon transfers that move wealth more than one generation below the transferor but that do not cause anyone in an intervening generation to become the owner for gift tax or estate tax purposes.

Almost immediately after the enactment of the Tax Reform Act of 1976, this writer perceived a consensus that the tax was unworkable and, therefore, doomed. The consensus became a prophecy, largely, in this writer's view, a self-fulfilling one. The prophecy culminated with the repeal and replacement of the tax. As much (or as little) as anything is permanent in the arena of federal taxation, the generation-skipping tax that presently is law apparently is here to stay. This writer does not detect that a consensus of unworkability applies to it. However, the real tests will come in the future when both tax practitioners and the government must turn their focus from conception to administration.

This second edition is the result of 17 years of thinking, arguing, lecturing, and writing about the generation-skipping tax, first that of the Tax Reform Act of 1976, and, since 1986, that of the Tax Reform Act of 1986. Among the dialogues, those with William M. Robinson, Jeffrey N. Pennell, Richard B. Covey, and the late A. James Casner were particularly provocative and, presumably, productive.

This book takes into account the proposed regulations that the Internal Revenue Service issued on December 24, 1992. It reflects, in its focus and emphasis, the treatment that the author anticipates will, and will not, become permanent.

Jerold I. Horn

Peoria, Illinois
December 1993

Contents

1

Introduction to the Generation-Skipping Tax

§ 1.01 BACKGROUND

A property owner often will want to give another person interests in, and powers over, property that approach those of outright ownership but that, *except to any extent the property is distributed to the other person* (or the other person absolutely can vest ownership in himself or herself), do not cause the other person to be the owner for income, gift, or estate tax purposes. A method commonly used to accomplish the objective is a transfer to a trust with one or more individuals having beneficial enjoyment but no individual (a) having any (i) general power of appointment or (ii) power exercisable solely by himself or herself to pay income to himself or herself, or (b) exercising any unrestricted power to transfer to any other person property in which he or she has a beneficial interest.[1] Until the advent of the generation-skipping tax ("GST") as part of the Tax Reform Act of 1976 ("TRA '76"), one or more persons could enjoy these connections successively with the property, including powers over it and interests in it, without attracting any transfer tax liability, for as long as the period of any applicable Rule Against Perpetuities.

[1] *See* Internal Revenue Code ("Code") §§ 2041, 2514, and 678(a)(1); Treas. Reg. §§ 25.2511-1(g)(2), 25.2511-1(h)(6), and 25.2514-1(b)(2); and Rev. Rul. 79-327, 1979-2 C.B. 342. All Code section references are to the Internal Revenue Code of 1986 unless otherwise indicated.

§ 1.02 THE THIRD TRANSFER TAX

TRA '76 superimposed upon these principles a third United States transfer tax, a generation-skipping tax. Generally, the purpose and the effect were to impose a United States transfer tax — a gift tax or an estate tax — or, if neither, a generation-skipping tax, upon the transfer of property (or an interest in it or a power over it) at least once at the level of each generation to which was assigned any person who had at least a possibility presently to benefit from the property (that is, a present "interest" in the property) or a power presently to establish or alter beneficial enjoyment of the property (that is, a present "power" over the property).[2] The intention was to neutralize the effect of trusts upon the frequency of the imposition of a transfer tax. Generally, the method of operation was to impose a tax substantially equivalent to the gift tax or estate tax that the property in question would have attracted if the property were owned outright (that is, at the time of the generation-skipping transfer) by a person (the "deemed transferor") in each successive generation in which (a) no person owned the property for gift tax or estate tax purposes, and (b) any person had any present interest in, or present power over, the property.[3]

§ 1.03 PRE-TRA '86 CALCULATION OF THE GENERATION-SKIPPING TAX

Calculation of the generation-skipping tax before the Tax Reform Act of 1986 ("TRA '86") was a five-step process.

First: Identify a "deemed transferor." By being deemed the transferor of the property that was included in the generation-skipping transfer, the deemed transferor was used only to determine the amount of the tax.

---

[2]A notable exception to this generality was that a taxable distribution could skip (without attracting a transfer tax) any one or more of the generations between (i) the highest generation below the grantor to which a person who had a present interest or a present power was assigned, and (ii) the generation to which the transferee was assigned, even if an individual assigned to any one or more of the intervening generations had a present interest or a present power.

[3]H.R. Rep. No. 94-1380, as to TRA '76 § 2006.

Second: Using the rate schedule of Code Section 2001(c), determine a tentative tax on the sum of all of the following transfers of, and attributed to, the deemed transferor:

i. The value of the property transferred in the particular generation-skipping transfer,

ii. The aggregate value of all prior generation-skipping transfers attributed to the deemed transferor (certain generation-skipping transfers occurring within three years before the deemed transferor died were treated under Code Section 2035 as occurring when the deemed transferor died),[4]

iii. The amount of adjusted taxable gifts made by the deemed transferor before the particular transfer, and

iv. If the deemed transferor died at the same time as, or before, the particular transfer, the taxable estate of the deemed transferor.[5]

Third: Using the same rate schedule, calculate a tentative tax on all of the foregoing transfers of, and attributed to, the deemed transferor other than the particular generation-skipping transfer.

Fourth: Subtract the tentative tax determined in step Third (that is, on all of the foregoing transfers of, and attributed to, the deemed transferor other than the particular transfer) from the tentative tax determined in step Second (that is, on all of the foregoing transfers of, and attributed to, the deemed transferor).

Fifth: Make certain adjustments, further to analogize the generation-skipping tax to the transfer tax that would have been payable if the deemed transferor had owned the property outright and transferred it during life or at death.[6]

§ 1.04 CRITICISM OF THE PRE-TRA '86 SYSTEM

The deemed transferor system, the pervasiveness of the tax, and the treatment of a power the same as an interest particularly attracted criticism.

---

[4]Pre-TRA '86 Code § 2602(e).

[5]Pre-TRA '86 Code § 2602(a).

[6]Pre-TRA '86 Code § 2602(c) and (d).

The Internal Revenue Service effectively admitted that it did not retain and could not create the records upon which the use of a deemed transferor's tax base depended. Theoretically, each and every generation-skipping trust, no matter how small at the outset, could have become involved with the tax. The concept of a "power" often was elusive, and a power in any event was a controversial nexus between a person and property to justify the imposition of a transfer tax. According to the critics, each of these concepts added significantly and unnecessarily to the complexity of the tax.

§ 1.05 REPEAL AND REPLACEMENT OF CHAPTER 13

The United States Treasury acceded to the repeal of Chapter 13 if, but only if, there was a replacement. TRA '86 repealed Chapter 13 retroactively to the date of its enactment and included a new Chapter 13.

2

Purpose and Effect of the Tax

§ 2.01 THE INTENDED PURPOSE

TRA '86 generally did not alter the gift tax or the estate tax. Rather, as had TRA '76, it superimposed a third transfer tax, a generation-skipping tax.

The policy objectives are considerably broader than those of Chapter 13 before TRA '86. The purpose that is popularly asserted is to impose a transfer tax, be it a gift tax or an estate tax or, if neither, a generation-skipping tax, upon the transfer of property (or an interest in it) at least once at the level of each generation, *regardless of whether any person assigned to a particular generation has any present interest or power.* Although the intention generally is to neutralize the effect of trusts upon the frequency of an imposition of a transfer tax, the tax applies even if the transfer that skips the first generation below the transferor is direct and not in trust.

§ 2.02 THE ACTUAL EFFECT

The actual effect appears to deviate substantially from the asserted purpose. The principal deviation is a function of the particular generation that is skipped. A second deviation is a function of statutory gaps, intended or inadvertent.

Generally, the effect is to impose a United States transfer tax, be it a gift tax or an estate tax or, if neither, a generation-skipping tax, upon the transfer of property (or an interest in it) (a) at the level of each generation two or more below the transferor to which is assigned any person who has any present interest in the property and (b) at the level of the generation one below the transferor, regardless of whether any person who is assigned to that generation has any present interest or power. A notable exception to this generality, discussed in § 8.03, *infra,* is that a taxable distribution can skip any one or more of the generations between (a) the generation one below the transferor and (b) the generation to which the transferee is assigned, even if an individual assigned to any one or more of the intervening generations has an interest.[1]

Another exception to this generality, also discussed in § 8.03, *infra,* is that a single event can cause a taxable termination that can skip any one or more of the generations between (i) the generation to which the non-skip person whose interest terminates is assigned and (ii) the generation to which the transferee is assigned, even if an individual assigned to any one or more of the intervening generations has an interest.[2]

Yet another exception to this generality is discussed in §§ 6.07, 6.09, and 8.04, *infra.* If a transfer is in trust, the transfer does not terminate any person's interest in any property held in a trust, and no person has an interest immediately after the transfer, but after the transfer a distribution (even, for example, a distribution on termination of the trust) may be made to a non-skip person, the transfer is not a direct skip or a taxable distribution (and is not otherwise a generation-skipping transfer) and, without attracting generation-skipping tax, can skip one or more generations. If a taxable termination is the first generation-skipping transfer that occurs after the transfer in trust, these "skippable" generations are the one or more generations *(including the first below the grantor)* between (a) the transferor and (b) the highest generation to which is assigned any person who has an interest before the taxable termination occurs. If, on the other hand, a taxable distribution is the first generation-skipping transfer that occurs after the transfer in trust, the one or more intervening generations between the generation one below the transferor and the generation to which the transferee is assigned are clearly skippable regardless of

---

[1] *Cf.* Prop. Treas. Reg. § 26.2612-1(f), Ex. 9, 57 Fed. Reg. 61362 (1992).

[2] Prop. Treas. Reg. § 26.2612-1(f), Ex. 9, 57 Fed. Reg. 61362 (1992).

whether any person assigned to any of these generations has an interest.[3]

§ 2.03 THE EFFECTIVE DATES

Generally, the generation-skipping tax applies to each "generation-skipping transfer" made after October 22, 1986.[4] However, there are important exceptions.

Any *inter vivos* transfer after September 25, 1985, and before October 23, 1986, is treated as if it were made on October 23, 1986. The tax is not applicable

i. To any generation-skipping transfer under a trust that was irrevocable on September 25, 1985, to such extent as the transfer is not from corpus added after September 25, 1985;

ii. To any generation-skipping transfer under a will executed before October 23, 1986, if the decedent died before 1987; or

iii. In the case of a decedent who on, and at all times after, October 22, 1986, was under a mental disability to change the disposition of his or her property, to any generation-skipping transfer, except to the extent the transfer is attributable to property transferred after August 3, 1990, to the decedent or the trust by gift or because of the death of another person, (a) under a trust, to the extent the trust is included in the decedent's gross estate for estate tax purposes, or (b) that is a direct skip that occurs because of the decedent's death.

---

[3] *Cf.* Prop. Treas. Reg. § 26.2612-1(f), Ex. 9, 57 Fed. Reg. 61362 (1992).

[4] TRA '86 § 1433(a).

3

The Taxable Events

§ 3.01 GENERATION-SKIPPING TRANSFERS

A generation-skipping tax is imposed upon every "generation-skipping transfer."[1]

The term "generation-skipping transfers" includes three taxable events:

a. Taxable distribution,
b. Taxable termination, and
c. Direct skip.[2]

Any generation-skipping transfer that otherwise would be classifiable as more than one type of taxable event shall be classified solely as the first of the following that applies:

a. Direct skip,
b. Taxable termination, and
c. Taxable distribution.[3]

§ 3.02 OTHER DEFINITIONS

An understanding of the taxable events requires familiarity with the defined terms that are used in their definitions.

§ 3.02(a) Skip Person

A "skip person" is (i) a natural person assigned to a generation that is two or more below the generation to which the transferor is

[1]Code § 2601.

[2]Code § 2611(a).

[3]*See* Prop. Treas. Reg. § 26.2612-1(b), (c), 57 Fed. Reg. 61361 (1992).

assigned or (ii) a trust in which (a) all interests are held by skip persons or (b) no interest is held by any person, and at no time after the transfer may distribution (including any distribution on termination) be made from the trust to a non-skip person.[4]

§ 3.02(b) Non-Skip Person

A non-skip person is any person who is not a skip person.[5]

§ 3.02(c) Generation Assignment

Generation assignment is determined by consanguinity or by age relative to the age of the transferor.

§ 3.02(c)(1) Lineal Descendants in General

An individual who is a descendant of a grandparent of the transferor is assigned to a generation, in relation to the transferor's, by comparing the number of generations from the grandparent to the individual with the number of generations (which is two) from the grandparent to the transferor.[6]

§ 3.02(c)(2) Lineal Descendants on the Spouse's Side

An individual (other than the transferor's spouse) who is a descendant of a grandparent of the transferor's spouse is assigned to a generation, again in relation to the transferor's, by comparing (a) the number of generations from the grandparent to the individual with (b) the number of generations (which is two) from the grandparent to the transferor's spouse.[7]

An individual (other than the transferor's former spouse) who is a descendant of a grandparent of the transferor's former spouse is assigned to a generation, again in relation to the transferor's, by comparing (a) the number of generations from the grandparent to the individual with (b) the number of generations (which is two) from the grandparent to the transferor's former spouse.[8]

---

[4]Code § 2613(a).

[5]Code § 2613(b).

[6]Code § 2651(b)(1).

[7]Code § 2651(b)(2).

[8]*Id.*

§ 3.02(c)(3) Marital Relationship

An individual who at any time has been married to a descendant of a grandparent of the transferor or of the transferor's spouse or of the transferor's former spouse is assigned to the spouse's generation; provided, that any such individual who at any time has been married to the transferor is assigned to the transferor's generation.[9]

§ 3.02(c)(4) Relatives Who Are Included

These rules determine the generation assignment of the following relatives of the transferor ("T"), and of the following relatives of the transferor's spouse ("TS"), and of the following relatives of the transferor's former spouse ("TFS"):

a. Grandparents ("GP"),

b. Parents ("P"),

c. Aunts ("A"),

d. Uncles ("U"),

e. Siblings ("B," "S"),

f. First Cousins ("1st C"),

g. Children ("C"),

h. Nieces ("N"),

i. Nephews ("N"),

j. First Cousins Once Removed ("1st C1R"),

k. Grandchildren ("GC"),

l. Grandnephews ("GN"),

m. Grandnieces ("GN"),

n. First Cousins Twice Removed ("1st C2R"),

o. The respective descendants (other than the transferor's spouse and the transferor's former spouse) of the foregoing persons, and,

p. The respective spouses of the transferor and the foregoing persons.

---

[9]Code § 2651(c).

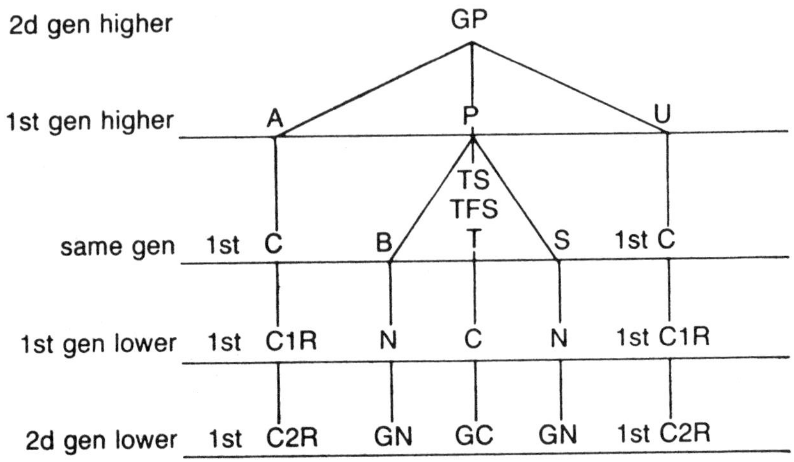

§ 3.02(c)(5) Rules for Determining Other Individuals' Generation Assignments

The generation assignment of any other individual is determined by comparing the date of birth of the individual to the date of birth of the transferor.[10] A generation consists of a 25-year interval. The first generation lower than the transferor includes individuals born more than 12½ years and not more than 37½ years after the transferor.

Any individual who on the basis of the foregoing is assigned to more than one generation shall be assigned to the lowest of these generations.[11] This rule may not apply in the case of an unrelated person who is adopted by, or married to, a descendant of the transferor's (or transferor's spouse's or transferor's former spouse's) grandparent. The consanguinity rules may govern that individual's assignment.[12]

When an entity has an interest, the one or more individuals having any interest through the entity (and not the entity itself)

---

[10]Code § 2651(d).

[11]Code § 2651(e)(1).

[12]*See* Former Prop. Treas. Reg. (withdrawn because of repeal of first version of Chapter 13) § 26.2611-3(c).

shall be treated as having the interest and shall be assigned according to the foregoing rules.[13]

§ 3.02(d) Transferor

§ 3.02(d)(1) In General

Generally, the "transferor" is (i) the decedent in the case of any property subject to estate tax or (ii) the donor in the case of any property subject to gift tax.[14] The transferor is the last person in whose gross estate or completed gifts (even if excluded from taxable gifts) the property was included.[15]

§ 3.02(d)(2) Splitting of Gifts

If the spouse of the actual donor is deemed for gift tax purposes (according to Code Section 2513(a)) to make one half of a gift, the spouse of the donor is treated for generation-skipping tax purposes as the transferor of that one half and the actual donor is treated for generation-skipping tax purposes as the transferor of the other one half.[16]

§ 3.02(d)(3) Special Election for Qualified Terminable Interest Property ("QTIP")

A person who creates qualified terminable interest property ("QTIP") can elect for generation-skipping tax purposes to treat the QTIP as if no QTIP election had been made. If the QTIP is includable in the completed gifts or gross estate of the donee or surviving spouse only because of a QTIP election, the election causes the spouse who creates the QTIP (rather than the donee or surviving spouse) to be the transferor for generation-skipping tax purposes.[17] The election is available only if it is made with respect to *all* of the property in the trust.

---

[13]Code § 2651(e)(2); Former Prop. Treas. Reg. (withdrawn because of repeal of first version of Chapter 13) § 26.2611-3(d) and (e).

[14]Code § 2652(a)(1).

[15]Code § 2652(a)(2).

[16]Prop. Treas. Reg. § 26.2652-1(a), 57 Fed. Reg. 61368 (1992).

[17]Code § 2652(a)(3).

§ 3.02(d)(4) Multiple Skip Transfers

If any property is transferred in a generation-skipping transfer and immediately after the transfer the transferred property is held in trust, for purposes of applying Chapter 13 (other than the rules concerning generation assignment) to subsequent transfers from the portion of the trust "attributable" to the transferred property,

> the trust will be treated as if the transferor of such property were assigned to the 1st generation above the highest generation of any person who has an interest in such trust immediately after the transfer.[18]

The rule applies only when a person has an interest in the trust immediately after a generation-skipping transfer. The rule does not apply if immediately after a generation-skipping transfer no one has an interest in the trust.

The proposed regulations address the omission: "If no person holds an interest in the trust immediately after the GST, the transferor is treated as occupying the generation above the highest generation of any person in existence at the time of the GST who may subsequently hold an interest in the trust."[19] Almost every trust that does not include an ultimate gift to charity and does not cause inclusion of a remainder interest in the completed gifts or gross estate of a remainder person before the remainder is possessory creates the possibility, however remote, that a non-skip person can have an interest in the future. Therefore, read literally, unless the trust includes an ultimate gift to charity, the proposed rule almost never will lower the transferor. While another rule, that of Code Section 2612(b)(2), might avoid a second generation-skipping transfer at the level of one generation, the proposed rule might imply that the contrary rule of Code Section 2612(b)(2) does not apply. This writer has suggested the remedy of including "immediately before the transfer was a skip person relative to the transferor and who" immediately after "who" and before "may" in the proposed rule.

§ 3.02(e) Interest

Generally, a person has an "interest" only if the person (i) has

---

[18] Code § 2653(a).

[19] Prop. Treas. Reg. § 26.2653-1(a), 57 Fed. Reg. 61370 (1992).

a right presently to receive, or (ii) is a permissible recipient presently of, income or corpus.[20]

§ 3.03 DIRECT SKIP

Generally, a "direct skip" is a transfer, subject to gift tax or estate tax, of an interest in property, to a skip person.[21]

Illustration 1:

During life or by will, a person gives $40,000 to the grandchild of his or her sibling.

Illustration 2:

Upon the death of a surviving spouse, the remainder of a QTIP trust (for which the surviving spouse is the "transferor" for purposes of the generation-skipping tax) passes to the grandchild of the transferor's sibling.

A direct skip occurs only with respect to property skipping the first generation below the transferor and only if no person in the first generation below the transferor has an interest.

Code Section 6166 permits deferral of generation-skipping tax upon direct skips that occur at the same time as, and because of, the death of the transferor.[22]

§ 3.04 TAXABLE TERMINATION

A "taxable termination" means the termination of an interest in property held in a trust, other than a direct skip, unless *immediately after the termination* (i) a non-skip person has an interest in the property or (ii) no person has any interest and at no time after the termination may a distribution (including distributions on termination) be made from the trust to a skip person.[23]

Illustration:

A property owner transfers property to a trustee for the trustee to pay the income to the grantor's child

[20]Code § 2652(c).

[21]Code § 2612(c).

[22]Code § 6166(i).

[23]Code § 2612(a).

until the death of the child, remainder to the grantor's grandchild if the grandchild survives the child.

If the grandchild survives the child, a taxable termination occurs upon the death of the child. Immediately after the termination of the child's interest, only a skip person (that is, the grandchild) has an interest.

§ 3.04(a) Different Concepts

Although the name, taxable termination, is the same in the TRA '86 version of Chapter 13 as in the TRA '76 version of Chapter 13, the concept is significantly different. A taxable termination can occur even if no person in any generation below the transferor has a present or, indeed, even a future interest. The possibility merely must exist that a skip person *will have an interest in the future.*

§ 3.04(b) Conditions for Occurrence

Subject to the separate share rules and the nominal interest rule, mentioned at §§ 3.04(b), (c), and (d), *infra,* when (i) more than one non-skip person has an interest in a trust, (ii) one non-skip person has more than one interest in a trust, or (iii) a non-skip person has an interest in a trust immediately after (although not immediately before) the termination of the interest of another non-skip person, a taxable termination cannot occur until the last interest terminates.[24] As a corollary, while any individual assigned to a particular generation continues to have an interest in a trust, no generation-skipping transfer can occur because of any termination of any nexus with the trust of any other individual assigned to the same or any lower generation.

Illustration 1:

More than one non-skip person has an interest:

A trustee is permitted to pay income and corpus from a single trust to any one or more children of the transferor until no living child is less than 21 years old.

---

[24]*See generally* Prop. Treas. Reg. § 26.2612-1(e), (f), Ex. 13, 57 Fed. Reg. 61362 (1992).

When no child is less than 21 years old, the trustee is to distribute the trust outright to the transferor's then-living descendants, per stirpes, without treating any prior distribution as an advancement. If a child dies survived by a descendant while a surviving child is less than 21 years old, a taxable termination does not occur until the trust terminates.

Illustration 2:

More than one non-skip person has an interest: A trustee is permitted to pay income and corpus to the transferor's spouse and child until the death of the spouse. When the spouse dies, the trustee is to distribute the trust outright to the child if living, otherwise to the child's then-living descendants, per stirpes. If the child dies before the spouse, a taxable termination does not occur until the death of the spouse.

Illustration 3:

One non-skip person has more than one interest: A trustee is permitted to distribute income and corpus to the transferor's descendants (consisting of a child and a grandchild) until the death of the child and the child has a power to withdraw 5 percent of the corpus per year, noncumulatively. Upon the child's death, the trustee must distribute the trust outright to the child's then-living descendants, per stirpes. A taxable termination does not occur until the child dies. Similarly, even if the child's only interest is the child's ability to withdraw 5 percent of corpus per year, noncumulatively, and the power exists for only a portion of each year, a taxable termination probably does not occur until the child dies.[25]

Illustration 4:

A non-skip person has an interest immediately after, but not before, termination of interest of another non-skip person:

[25] Former Prop. Treas. Reg. (withdrawn because of repeal of first version of Chapter 13) § 26.2613-2(c)(2).

A trustee must pay income to the transferor's child until the death of the child. Subject to the child's exercise of a nongeneral, testamentary power of appointment, the principal will pass to the child's descendants, per stirpes, living at the child's death. The child exercises the power to pay the trust income to the surviving spouse of the child for life, with the principal to pass at the spouse's death to the child's then-living descendants, per stirpes. A taxable termination does not occur until the death of the child's spouse.

§ 3.04(c) Shares Treated as Separate Trusts

If more than one individual has an interest in a single trust and different individuals have substantially separate and independent shares, the shares are treated as separate trusts.[26] The termination of a particular individual's last interest in a separate share may be a taxable termination even if a non-skip person has or continues to have an interest in another share. The normal rules for a taxable termination may not apply with respect to the entire trust but may apply with respect to a separate share.[27]

A portion of a trust that for income tax purposes is treated according to Code Section 663(c) as a separate trust will be treated also for generation-skipping tax purposes as a separate trust if, but only if, "the share exists from and after the creation of the trust, that is, the date of death of the grantor if the trust is includible in its entirety in the grantor's gross estate for Federal estate tax purposes."[28]

A rule that is not a separate share rule produces a result, concerning timing of the transfer, that is similar to the result of the separate share rule that applies to substantially separate and independent shares of different individuals. If, upon the death of a descendant of the transferor, the descendant's interest terminates and a portion of the trust "peels off" and is distributed to, or to a

---

[26]Code § 2654(b)(2).

[27]Code § 2654(b); *cf.* Former Prop. Treas. Reg. (withdrawn because of repeal of first version of Chapter 13) § 26.2613-5(a).

[28]Prop. Treas. Reg. § 26.2654-1(b)(2), 57 Fed. Reg. 61370 (1992).

trust for, one or more skip persons, the termination is a taxable termination with respect to the "peeled-off" portion.[29]

§ 3.04(d) Transferors' Portions Treated as Separate Trusts

A separate share rule also applies if a single trust has more than one transferor. The portion attributable to each transferor is treated as a separate trust.[30]

§ 3.04(e) Disregard of Certain Interests

Additionally, functionally similar to the separate share rules, an interest that is used "primarily" to postpone or avoid any generation-skipping tax will be ignored.[31] The proposed regulations announce a harsher test, arguably without any statutory foundation for it. "If a significant purpose for the creation of an interest in trust is to postpone or avoid the GST tax, the interest is disregarded for purposes of chapter 13. The creation of an interest in a trust may have more than one significant purpose."[32] By contrast, an interest only can have one "primary" use or purpose.

§ 3.05 TAXABLE DISTRIBUTION

A "taxable distribution" is any distribution from a trust to a skip person other than a taxable termination or a direct skip.[33]

Illustration:

A property owner transfers property to a trustee and empowers the trustee to pay income to any one or more of the grantor's spouse and descendants or to accumulate it, and to pay principal to any one or more of the grantor's spouse and descendants, until the death of the grantor's spouse, remainder to the grantor's then-living descendants, per stirpes.

---

[29]Code § 2612(a)(2).

[30]Code § 2654(b)(1).

[31]Code § 2652(c)(2).

[32]Prop. Treas. Reg. § 26.2612-1(e)(2)(ii), 57 Fed. Reg. 61361 (1992).

[33]Code § 2612(b).

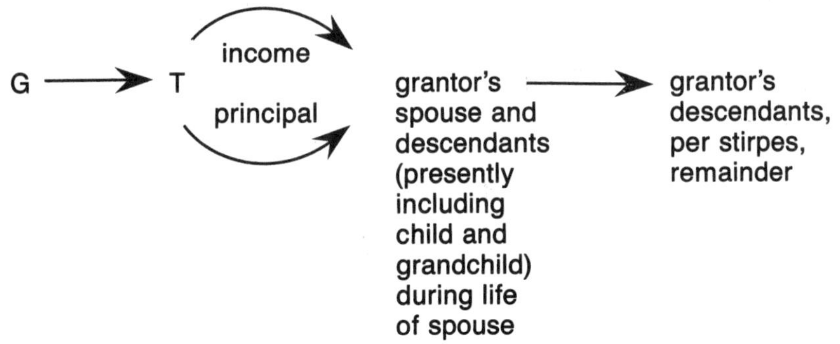

Any distribution (that is, of income or principal), other than (according to the proposed regulations) a distribution that terminates all interest of the spouse and the child in the trust, during the life of the grantor's spouse to the grantor's grandchild is a taxable distribution. The distribution is from a trust, and the grandchild is a skip person. If the distribution terminated all interest of the spouse and the child in the trust, the proposed regulations would classify it as a taxable termination rather than a taxable distribution, notwithstanding that the distribution was discretionary rather than mandatory.[34]

§ 3.05(a) Different Concepts

Although the name, taxable distribution, is the same in the TRA '86 version of Chapter 13 as in the TRA '76 version of Chapter 13, the concept is significantly different. A taxable distribution can occur even if no person in any generation below the transferor but above the transferee has any present interest.

Illustration:

Assume the existence of the trust described in the preceding illustration, except that no child survived the creation of the trust.

---

[34]*See* Prop. Treas. Reg. § 26.2612-1(f), Ex. 8, 57 Fed. Reg. 61362 (1992).

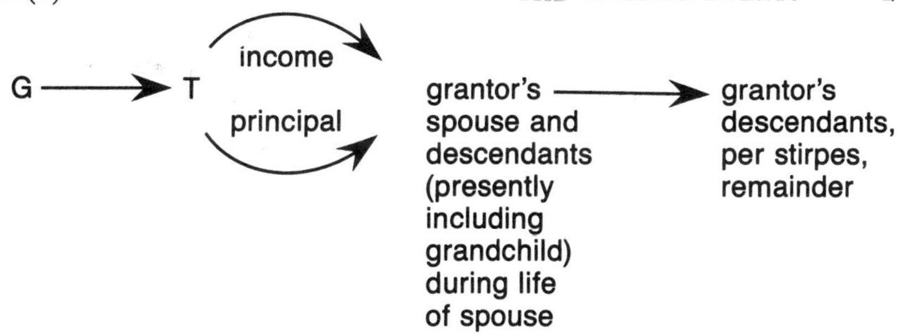

Any distribution to the grandchild during the life of the spouse of the grantor, other than (according to the proposed regulations) a distribution that terminates all interest of the spouse in the trust, is a taxable distribution even though no child has any interest.

§ 3.05(b) Below-Market Loans

Loans that bear below-market interest (and, impliedly, use of property upon payment of below-market rent or other charges) can be distributions.[35]

§ 3.06 EXCEPTIONS

Exceptions prevent certain transfers from being generation-skipping transfers. The exceptions relate to multiple applications of transfer tax, transfers that are excludable for gift tax purposes, and direct skips.

§ 3.06(a) Multiple Applications of Transfer Tax

Chapter 13 prevents multiple applications of transfer tax in some situations. The definition of "transferor" is designed to coordinate the application of the generation-skipping tax with the application of the gift tax and the estate tax. The inclusion of trust property in an individual's completed gifts or gross estate causes the individual to become the "transferor" (for generation-skipping tax purposes) of the property so included.[36] This causes the new transferor and certain other persons to be non-skip persons and thus causes certain transfers not to be generation-skipping trans-

[35]Former Prop. Treas. Reg. (withdrawn because of repeal of first version of Chapter 13) § 26.2613-1(f)(1); *cf.* Code § 7872.

[36]Code § 2652(a)(1).

fers. This mechanism should prevent a single transfer from attracting a generation-skipping tax at the level of any generation at which it attracts a gift tax or an estate tax. Conversely, that a transfer is subject to a gift tax or estate tax at the level of any particular generation that is more than one generation below the transferor does not mean that the property escapes a generation-skipping tax as it passes through the one or more intervening generations below the transferor.

Two other provisions, partly overlapping, are designed to control the frequency of application of the generation-skipping tax, *per se*.

First, generation-skipping transfer

> does not include . . . any transfer to the extent —
>
> (A) the property transferred was subject to a prior [generation-skipping tax],
>
> (B) the transferee in the prior transfer was assigned to the same generation as (or a lower generation than) the generation assignment of the transferee in this transfer, and
>
> (C) such transfers do not have the effect of avoiding [generation-skipping tax] with respect to any transfer.[37]

Second, after certain generation-skipping transfers, the generation to which the transferor is assigned is lowered, and this causes certain persons to be non-skip persons and thus causes certain transfers not to be generation-skipping transfers.[38]

Illustration:

Assume that a gift to a trust is a generation-skipping transfer because only the transferor's grandnephew has an interest immediately after the transfer. Assume, further, that during the grandnephew's life the trustee is directed to pay income to the grandnephew, and not to distribute principal and that upon the death of the grandnephew the remaining property passes to the transferor's grandniece.

---

[37]Code § 2611(b)(2); *cf.* Former Prop. Treas. Reg. (withdrawn because of repeal of first version of Chapter 13) § 26.2613-4(b)(2).

[38]Code § 2653(a); Prop. Treas. Reg. § 26.2653-1(a), 57 Fed. Reg. 61370 (1992).

If these provisions did not exist, (i) the passage of the property to another skip person (that is, the grandniece) in the same generation because of the termination of the interest of the first skip person (that is, the grandnephew) could be a second generation-skipping transfer, in the form of a taxable termination, at the level of the same generation, and (ii) a distribution from the trust to the grandnephew could be a second generation-skipping transfer, in the form (according to the proposed regulations) of a taxable distribution if the distribution does not terminate all interest of the grandnephew in the trust or a taxable termination if the distribution does terminate all interest of the grandnephew in the trust. Either of these provisions, alone, seems sufficient to prevent the second generation-skipping transfer.

§ 3.06(b) Exceptions for Exclusions from Taxable Gifts

Two exceptions parallel those that are available for gift tax purposes.

First, certain gifts that are excluded from taxable gifts because of annual exclusions for gifts of present interests, taking into account gift-splitting permitted by Code Section 2513(a), are exempt from the generation-skipping tax. With respect to transfers after March 31, 1988, this exemption automatically affects the inclusion ratio, not the tax base.[39] It is available only for direct skips that in all events are includable in the donee's transfer tax base. An annual exclusion gift to a trust after March 31, 1988, automatically has an inclusion ratio of zero only if the (i) trust property is not distributable to any person other than the donee during the life of the donee, and (ii) the trust property is includable in the donee's gross estate for estate tax purposes if the trust does not terminate before the donee dies.

Second, generation-skipping transfer does not include any transfer that, if made by an individual during life, would be a "qualified transfer" excluded from taxable gifts according to Code Section 2503(e).[40]

[39] Code § 2642(c).

[40] Code § 2611(b)(1).

§ 3.06(c) Direct Skip Exception

Last, the statute contained two exceptions, and it continues to contain one exception, from the concept of a direct skip.

§ 3.06(c)(1) Grandchild Exclusion

First, a "direct skip" did not include any transfer before 1990 to a grandchild of the transferor except to any extent that the aggregate of the transfers to the grandchild exceeded $2,000,000.[41]

a. The transfer, but for the exclusion, must have been a direct skip.
b. The transferor (that is, not the transferor's spouse or former spouse) must have been the grandparent.
c. The transfer must have been "to" the grandchild. A transfer in trust was a transfer "to" the grandchild if, and only if,
    i. the trust property was not distributable to any person other than the grandchild during the life of the grandchild,
    ii. the trust property was includable in the gross estate of the grandchild for estate tax purposes if the grandchild died before the trust terminated, and
    iii. with respect to transfers after June 10, 1987, all trust income was distributable currently (that is, at least annually) to the grandchild after the grandchild attained 21 years of age.

If the exclusion was the only reason that a direct skip (and thus a "generation-skipping transfer") did not occur upon a transfer to a trust, the statute "deemed" it to occur for purposes of subsequent application of Chapter 13 to the trust. This mechanism causes Code Section 2653(a) to operate to lower the generation assignment of the transferor. The lowering of the generation assignment of the transferor prevents a distribution of the transferred property from the trust to the transferee grandchild from being a distribution to a skip person and thus a taxable distribution.

§ 3.06(c)(2) Predeceased Child Exception

Second, solely for purposes of determining the occurrence of a "direct skip," if the transferor survives the one or more descendants

[41] TRA '86 § 1433(b)(3).

of the transferor (or of the transferor's spouse or former spouse) who occupy the generations immediately below the generation of the transferor, the descendants of the deceased descendants ascend to occupy the "open" generations. For example, a grandchild of the transferor (or of the transferor's spouse or former spouse) is treated as a child of the transferor (and the generation assignment of each descendant of the child is raised one) if at the time of the transfer the grandchild's parent who is a child of the transferor (or of the transferor's spouse or former spouse) is deceased.[42]

Mechanically, the grandchild is treated as a child (and the grandchild's child is treated as a grandchild), for purposes of determining the occurrence of a direct skip. The transfer, but for the exception, must be a direct skip. If the predeceased child exception is the only reason that a transfer to a trust is not a direct skip, the generation assignment that applies for purposes of the predeceased child exception applies also for purposes of determining the occurrence of generation-skipping transfers from the portion of the trust attributable to that property.

[42]Code § 2612(c)(2); Prop. Treas. Reg. § 26.2612-1(a)(2), 57 Fed. Reg. 61361 (1992).

4

Amount of Transfer

§ 4.01 THE TAXABLE AMOUNT IN GENERAL

The "taxable amount" is the base to which the tax applies. The amount of generation-skipping tax payable is (a) the "taxable amount," which is determined as described in this chapter, multiplied by (b) the "applicable rate," which is determined as discussed in Chapter 5, *infra.*[1]

§ 4.02 TAXABLE AMOUNT — TAXABLE DISTRIBUTION

The taxable amount in the case of a taxable distribution is (a) the value of the property received by the transferee, minus (b) any expense incurred in connection with the determination, collection, or refund of the generation-skipping tax with respect to the transfer.[2]

> ***Illustration:***
>
> **A property owner transfers property to a discretionary trust for the benefit of the grantor's descendants until the death of the grantor's child. During the life of the child, the trustee distributes $1,000,000, being one fourth of the trust estate, to the grantor's grandchild. The transferee pays a lawyer $1,000 to determine the generation-skipping tax. The taxable amount in the case of this taxable distribution is $999,000.**

---

[1]Code § 2602.

[2]Code § 2621(a).

Similar to the estate tax but contrary to the gift tax, the tax base of a taxable distribution includes the tax itself. Conceptually, the taxable distribution consists of two parts: One part is the tax, and the other part is the after-tax amount that the transferee can retain.

The transferee is liable for payment of the tax.[3] If any of the tax is paid from the trust, an amount equal to the tax so paid is, itself, a taxable distribution.[4] The additional distribution is regarded as occurring on the last day of the calendar year in which the original distribution is made.[5]

§ 4.03 TAXABLE AMOUNT — TAXABLE TERMINATION

The taxable amount in the case of a taxable termination is (a) the value of the property with respect to which the taxable termination has occurred, minus (b) certain items, similar to the expenses, debts, and taxes for which a deduction is allowed under Code Section 2053, attributable to the subject of the taxable termination.[6]

Illustration:

A property owner transfers $1,000,000 to a trustee to pay income to the grantor's child until the death of the child. Upon the child's death, the property, still $1,000,000, passes to the grantor's grandchild. The trustee pays itself a termination fee of $50,000. The taxable amount in the case of this taxable termination is $950,000.

Similar to the estate tax but contrary to the gift tax, the tax base of a taxable termination includes the tax itself. Conceptually, the "property with respect to which the taxable termination has occurred" consists of two parts: One part is the tax, and the other part is the after-tax amount that the trust or the transferee can retain.

The trustee is liable for payment of the tax.[7]

---

[3]Code § 2603(a)(1).

[4]Code § 2621(b).

[5]Prop. Treas. Reg. § 26.2612-1(c), 57 Fed. Reg. 61361 (1992).

[6]Code § 2622.

[7]Code § 2603(a)(2).

The "property with respect to which the taxable termination has occurred" is all of the property from which an interest *could have been* (not necessarily was) satisfied.[8] An insignificant interest can produce a significant taxable amount. Consider, for example, an interest consisting of:

a. A right to withdraw $5,000 (or, alternatively, the greater of $5,000 and 5 percent of the trust corpus) per calendar year, noncumulatively, from a trust which has a corpus of $10,000,000, that is, an amount vastly greater than the amount subject to be withdrawn;
b. A right to receive income and corpus pursuant to an ascertainable standard relating to the beneficiary's health, education, or support, considering resources otherwise available, when the beneficiary's own resources make the chance of any payment unlikely but not so remote as to be negligible;
c. An ability to receive income and corpus in the trustee's broad discretion; and
d. A right of an 85-year old person to receive trust income commencing at age 85.

§ 4.04 TAXABLE AMOUNT — DIRECT SKIP

The taxable amount in the case of a direct skip is the value of the property received by the transferee.[9]

Illustration:

A widow previously exhausted her ability to make nontaxable gifts to her grandnephew. The widow now gives $100,000 to the grandnephew. The taxable amount of this direct skip is $100,000.

Similar to the gift tax but contrary to the estate tax, the generation-skipping tax base of a direct skip does not include the tax itself. However, any generation-skipping tax imposed on the

[8] *Cf.* Conf. Rep., as to TRA '76 § 2006; and Former Prop. Treas. Reg. (withdrawn because of repeal of first version of Chapter 13) § 26.2613-3(b).

[9] Code § 2623.

transferor with respect to a taxable gift that also is a direct skip is an additional gift.[10] Any generation-skipping tax imposed with respect to a direct skip from the transferor's taxable estate is already included in the transferor's taxable estate. Therefore, it should not, and does not, increase the taxable estate.

If the direct skip is from a trust, the trustee is liable for payment of the tax.[11] If the direct skip is not from a trust, the transferor is liable for payment of the tax.[12]

§ 4.05 VALUE FOR PURPOSES OF DETERMINING TAXABLE AMOUNT

Generally, property shall be valued for generation-skipping tax purposes at the time of the transfer.[13] The value of any direct skip included in the transferor's gross estate shall be the value of the property for estate tax purposes.[14] Alternate valuation is available if the election will decrease the sum of estate tax and generation-skipping tax payable with respect to property included in the gross estate.[15] Special use valuation for this property is available under Code Section 2032A. If one or more taxable terminations occur upon, and as a result of, the death of an individual, alternate valuation of the property included in the terminations is available.[16] Any consideration that a transferee pays offsets the value of any generation-skipping transfer.[17]

---

[10] Code § 2515.

[11] Code § 2603(a)(2).

[12] Code § 2603(a)(3).

[13] Code § 2624(a).

[14] Code § 2624(b).

[15] Code § 2032(c)(2).

[16] Code § 2624(c).

[17] Code § 2624(d).

5

Calculation of Tax

§ 5.01 IN GENERAL

The amount of generation-skipping tax payable with respect to the particular generation-skipping transfer is the "taxable amount," which is determined as discussed in Chapter 4, multiplied by the "applicable rate," which is determined as described in this chapter.[1]

§ 5.02 THE APPLICABLE RATE

The applicable rate is the maximum United States estate tax rate with respect to estates of decedents dying at the time of the particular generation-skipping transfer, multiplied by the "inclusion ratio" with respect to the transfer.[2]

§ 5.02(a) The Inclusion Ratio

§ 5.02(a)(1) In General

Except as otherwise defined in § 5.02(a)(2), the inclusion ratio is one, minus the "applicable fraction" determined for the trust or, as the case may be, the direct skip.[3]

§ 5.02(a)(2) Ratio for Certain Direct Skips That Are Nontaxable Gifts

In the case of

[1]Code § 2602.

[2]Code § 2641; see § 5.02(a), *infra.*

[3]Code § 2642(a)(1).

i. A direct skip, which is a nontaxable, outright gift,

ii. A nontaxable gift before April 1, 1988, which is the first transfer to the trust, or

iii. An annual exclusion gift after March 31, 1988, to a trust, which in all events is includable in the gross estate of the donee at the death of the donee or is paid to or for the donee during the life of the donee,

the inclusion ratio is zero.[4]

A nontaxable gift is any transfer to the extent the transfer is excluded from taxable gifts. Gifts of present interests described in Code Section 2503(b), after allowing for gift splitting according to Code Section 2513(a), are excluded from taxable gifts. Transfers that, if made by individuals, would be qualified transfers described in Code Section 2503(e) are excluded from taxable gifts.

§ 5.02(b) The Applicable Fraction

§ 5.02(b)(1) In General

The applicable fraction is a fraction determined for the trust from or in which a transfer occurs, or determined for a direct skip.

Except in the case of property transferred to a charitable lead annuity trust after October 13, 1987:

a. The numerator is the amount of the GST exemption allocated to the trust (or, as the case may be, to the property transferred in the direct skip).[5]

b. The denominator is the value (generally as of the time of the transfer to the trust or, as the case may be, the direct skip) of the property transferred to the trust (or, as the case may be, involved in the direct skip), not including any nontaxable gift made before April 1, 1988, minus the sum of

---

[4]Code § 2642(c)(1), (2)(B).

[5]Code § 2642(a)(2).

i. Any United States estate tax that is chargeable to, and actually recovered from, the trust,

ii. Any state death tax that is chargeable to, and actually recovered from, the trust,

iii. Any charitable deduction allowed for gift tax or estate tax purposes for property transferred to the trust, and[6]

iv. In the case of a direct skip, the value of the portion that is a nontaxable gift.

§ 5.02(b)(2) Special Rules for Charitable Lead Annuity Trusts

For purposes of determining the inclusion ratio of property transferred to a charitable lead annuity trust after October 13, 1987:

a. The numerator is the sum of (i) the amount of the GST exemption allocated to the trust and (ii) interest on the amount at (i), determined for the duration of the charitable lead annuity (but if the allocation of GST exemption is late, only from the date of allocation) at the rate that was used to determine the deduction for the charitable lead annuity.[7]

b. The denominator is the value of the property in the trust immediately after the termination of the charitable lead annuity.[8]

§ 5.03 ALGEBRAIC EXPRESSION

Expressed algebraically,

$X = TA \times AR$, when

X = The amount of generation-skipping tax payable with respect to the particular generation-skipping transfer,

---

[6] *Id.;* Prop. Treas. Reg. § 26.2642-1(c), 57 Fed. Reg. 61365 (1992).

[7] Code § 2642(e); Prop. Treas. Reg. § 26.2642-3, 57 Fed. Reg. 61366 (1992).

[8] Code § 2642(e).

TA = The taxable amount, and
AR = The applicable rate.

$AR = MR \times IR$, when

AR = The applicable rate,
MR = The maximum estate tax rate at the time of the generation-skipping transfer, and
IR = The inclusion ratio.

If the particular transfer is (i) a direct skip that is a nontaxable, outright gift, (ii) a nontaxable gift before April 1, 1988, that is the first transfer to the trust, or (iii) an annual exclusion gift after March 31, 1988, to a trust that in all events is includable in the gross estate of the donee at the death of the donee or is paid to or for the donee during the life of the donee, $IR = 0$. In all other cases, $IR = 1 - AF$, when

IR = The inclusion ratio, and
AF = The applicable fraction.

Except in the case of property transferred to a charitable lead annuity trust after October 13, 1987:

$$AF = \frac{GST}{VP - (USDT + SDT + CD + NT)}, \text{ when}$$

AF = The applicable fraction,
GST = The amount of GST exemption allocated to the trust (or, as the case may be, to the property transferred in the direct skip),
VP = The value of property transferred to the trust (or, as the case may be, involved in the direct skip), not including any nontaxable gift made before April 1, 1988,
USDT = Any United States death tax that is chargeable to, and actually recovered from, the trust,
SDT = Any state death tax that is chargeable to, and actually recovered from, the trust,
CD = Any charitable deduction allowed for gift tax or estate tax purposes for property transferred to the trust, and

NT = In the case of a direct skip, the value of the portion of the transfer that is a nontaxable gift.

For purposes of determining the inclusion ratio of property transferred to a charitable lead annuity trust after October 13, 1987:

$$AF = \frac{GST + I}{VPAT}, \text{ when}$$

AF = The applicable fraction,

GST = The amount of GST exemption allocated to the trust,

I = The interest on GST for the duration of the charitable lead annuity (but if the allocation of GST exemption is late, only from the date of allocation) at the rate used to determine the deduction for the charitable lead annuity, and

VPAT = The value of property in the trust immediately after the termination of the charitable lead annuity.

Collapsing the formulae and using the same nomenclature,

$$X = TA\ (MR\ (1 - \frac{GST}{VP - (USDT + SDT + CD + NT)}))$$

or, in the case of property transferred after October 13, 1987, to a charitable lead annuity trust,

$$X = TA\ (MR\ (1 - \frac{(GST + I)}{VPAT})).$$

The first component, X, is the unknown for which the formula is being solved. The second component, TA, is the amount of the particular transfer (that is, the base upon which the tax is imposed). The third component, the applicable rate,

$$(MR\ (1 - \frac{GST}{VP - (USDT + SDT + CD + NT)}))$$

or, as the case may be,

$$(MR\ (1 - \frac{(GST + I)}{VPAT})),$$

solely produces a fraction or percentage. An increase in GST reduces the percentage, and a decrease in GST increases the percentage.

§ 5.04 CREDIT

If a taxable termination occurs at the same time as, and because of, the death of an individual, a credit against United States generation-skipping tax is available for generation-skipping tax paid to any state with respect to the transfer (but not in excess of 5 percent of the United States generation-skipping tax calculated without the credit).[9]

§ 5.05 GST EXEMPTION

§ 5.05(a) The General Rule

Each individual is allowed a GST exemption of $1,000,000.[10] A transferor owns the exemption and cannot transfer it. However, the transferor (or the transferor's executor) can allocate the exemption to any property of which the possessor is the transferor.[11] According to the Code, the exemption is allocable to "property." According to the proposed regulations, if the allocation is with respect to property held in trust, the allocation is to the entire trust rather than to particular property in the trust.[12] The important point, in either case, is that the exemption is not allocable to a generation-skipping transfer. This means that the exemption is available with respect to all of the transferor's transfers of the particular property, regardless of the number of transfers and regardless of changes of value. Any allocation is irrevocable.[13]

§ 5.05(b) Affirmative Allocation of the Exemption

An individual (or the individual's executor) is permitted to allocate any GST exemption on or before the date upon which a timely filed estate tax return is required to be filed (or, if not

[9] Code § 2604.

[10] Code § 2631(a).

[11] *Id.*

[12] Prop. Treas. Reg. § 26.2632-1(a), 57 Fed. Reg. 61362 (1992).

[13] Code § 2631(b).

required to be filed, would be required to be filed if required).[14] A transferor and a transferor's executor can allocate GST exemption by means of a formula.[15]

§ 5.05(c) Default Allocation of the Exemption

If the transferor (or the transferor's executor) fails to allocate, the statute provides a "default" procedure.

§ 5.05(c)(1) Transfers During Transferor's Life

Subject to an individual's election to the contrary, any previously unallocated portion of the individual's GST exemption shall be allocated to the property transferred in any direct skip that the individual makes during life, thus (if the unused portion is sufficient) making the inclusion ratio zero.[16] A transferor who wishes to avoid automatic allocation must file a timely gift tax return that indicates by description or by payment of tax the extent to which the automatic allocation is not to apply.[17]

Until the advent of the proposed regulations, if the unified credit of the donor was sufficient to absorb all liability for gift tax, the splitting of gifts by means of a late-filed return did not produce any penalty. Generally, according to Code Section 2513(a) and its regulations, a donor and the donor's spouse can split their gifts to third persons during any year by signifying their consent on the last gift tax return timely filed for the gifts or on the first gift tax return late-filed for the gifts. According to Code Section 2652(a)(2), the splitting of gifts between spouses for gift tax purposes causes the actual donor to be the transferor of one half of the gift and the deemed donor to be the transferor of the other half.

According to Section 26.2632-1(b)(1)(ii) of the proposed regulations,[18] a timely filed gift tax return is necessary to prevent the automatic allocation of GST exemption to direct skips that a transferor makes during life. Therefore, failure to split a direct skip for

---

[14] Code § 2632(a)(1).

[15] Prop. Treas. Reg. § 26.2632-1(b)(2), (d), 57 Fed. Reg. 61363-64 (1992).

[16] Code § 2632(b).

[17] Prop. Treas. Reg. § 26.2632-1(b), 57 Fed. Reg. 61362-63 (1992).

[18] 57 Fed. Reg. 61363 (1992).

gift (and generation-skipping) tax purposes upon a timely return results in automatic allocation of the donor's GST exemption to all of the gift that is not an exempt, nontaxable gift. Presumably, the subsequent, late filing of a gift tax return splits the gift for both gift tax and generation-skipping tax purposes. The split changes the transferor of one half of the direct skip for generation-skipping tax purposes. Also, depending upon the configuration, the split can increase the amount of the gift that is nontaxable and exempt. Unless the deemed transferor affirmatively makes a late allocation of GST exemption at the time that the gift is split (using values current at the time of the late filing), the change of transferor seems to generate liability for generation-skipping tax. The change of transferor additionally might waste one half (or more) of the prior, automatic allocation of the original transferor.[19]

§ 5.05(c)(2) Transfers at or After Transferor's Death

Any portion of an individual's GST exemption that is not allocated within the permitted time after the individual's death is allocated for the individual. First, the unallocated exemption is allocated to property that is transferred in a direct skip at the individual's death. Second, any remaining portion of the unallocated exemption is allocated to trusts with respect to which the individual is the transferor and from which a taxable distribution or taxable termination is possible at or after the individual's death.[20] Each of these successive allocations is in proportion to the nonexempt portions (at the time of allocation) of the subject properties or trusts.[21] The "nonexempt portion" is

> The value (at the time of allocation) of the property or trust, multiplied by
>
> The inclusion ratio with respect to the property or trust.[22]

---

[19]Prop. Treas. Reg. § 26-2632-1(b)(1), 57 Fed. Reg. 61362-63 (1992).

[20]Code § 2632(c)(1).

[21]Code § 2632(c)(2)(A).

[22]Code § 2632(c)(2)(B).

No GST exemption automatically is allocated to any trust that will have a new transferor before a generation-skipping transfer can occur, as, for example, qualified terminable interest property for which a reverse QTIP election is not made according to Code Section 2652(a)(3).[23]

§ 5.05(d) The Valuation Rules

§ 5.05(d)(1) Value if Gift Tax Return Is Timely Filed or Allocation Is Deemed Made

If any GST exemption is (i) allocated on a gift tax return that is timely filed (or, if not required to be filed, would be timely if required) to property that is transferred during the life of the transferor or (ii) deemed allocated (according to Code Section 2632(b)(1)) to property transferred in a direct skip during the transferor's life, the value of the transferred property for purposes of determining its inclusion ratio is its value for gift tax purposes, and the allocation is effective on and after the date of the transfer.[24]

§ 5.05(d)(2) Value if Gift Tax Return Is Not Timely Filed

If any allocation of the GST exemption is made during the transferor's life on a gift tax return that is not timely filed (or, if not required to be filed, would not be timely if required) and is not deemed made according to Code Section 2632(b)(1), the value of the transferred property for purposes of determining its inclusion ratio is its value as of the time the allocation is filed (or, except in the case of life insurance, upon election is its value as of the first day of the month in which the allocation is filed), and the allocation is effective on and after the date the allocation is filed (or, except in the case of life insurance, upon election is effective on the first day of the month in which the election is filed).[25] If any allocation of the GST exemption is made after the transferor's death with respect to a transfer during the transferor's life for which a gift tax return would not be timely, the executor makes the allocation

[23]Prop. Treas. Reg. § 26.2632-1(d)(2), 57 Fed. Reg. 61364 (1992).

[24]Code § 2642(b)(1).

[25]Code § 2642(b)(3); Prop. Treas. Reg. § 26.2642-2(a)(2), 57 Fed. Reg. 61365 (1992).

on the estate tax return, and the allocation is effective as of the transferor's death.[26]

§ 5.05(d)(3) Value if Property Is Transferred at or After Transferor's Death

If any GST exemption is (i) allocated on a timely filed estate tax return to property that is transferred as a result of the transferor's death (or that is qualified terminable interest property that is deemed transferred according to Code Section 2044 and of which the surviving spouse is the transferor for generation-skipping tax purposes) or (ii) deemed allocated according to Code Section 2632(c), the value of the transferred property for purposes of determining its inclusion ratio is its value for estate tax purposes,[27] and the allocation is effective on and after the date of death of the transferor.[28] However, the Code says that if post-death appreciation and depreciation are not allocated to a particular disposition according to the regulations, the value of the transferred property for purposes of determining the inclusion ratio shall be determined as of the date of the distribution of the property.[29] See Appendix, Form #4, *infra.* The legislative history, citing Revenue Procedure 64-19,[30] indicated that the regulations would require ratable allocation of appreciation and depreciation in the value of all property available for distribution. According to the proposed regulations, if for generation-skipping tax purposes property is to be allocated to a particular disposition at its value for estate tax purposes, the system of funding must require ratable sharing of appreciation and depreciation. Conversely, if the system of funding does not require ratable sharing of appreciation and depreciation, the date of distribution values shall control for purposes of the allocation.[31]

---

[26]Prop. Treas. Reg. § 26.2632-1(d), 57 Fed. Reg. 61364 (1992).

[27]Code § 2642(b)(2)(A), (b)(4).

[28]Code § 2642(b)(2)(B).

[29]Code § 2642(b)(2)(A).

[30]1964-1 C.B. 682.

[31]Prop. Treas. Reg. § 26.2642-2(b)(2), (3), 57 Fed. Reg. 61365-66 (1992).

§ 5.05(e) Special Rules for Certain *Inter Vivos* Transfers

Special rules, exceptions to those previously discussed, apply with respect to lifetime transfers of property that would be included in the transferor's gross estate for estate tax purposes (other than because of Code Section 2035) if the transferor died immediately after making the transfer. According to the Code, no allocation of GST exemption to this property is effective until the earliest of (i) the time the property would not be includable in the transferor's gross estate if the transferor died, (ii) the occurrence of a generation-skipping transfer with respect to the property, and (iii) the death of the transferor.[32] Additionally, "[e]xcept as provided in regulations, any reference in this subsection [(f)] to an individual or transferor shall be treated as including a reference to the spouse of such individual or transferor."[33]

According to Section 26.2632-1(c)(2) of the proposed regulations.[34]

> (2) *Estate tax inclusion period defined.* An ETIP is the period during which, should death occur, the value of transferred property would be includible (other than by reason of section 2035) in the gross estate of —
> (i) The transferor;
> (ii) The transferor had the transferor retained an interest held by the transferor's spouse (but only to the extent the spouse acquired the interest from the transferor in an inter vivos transfer that was not included in the transferor's taxable gifts or for which a deduction was allowed under section 2523 of the Code); or
> (iii) The spouse of the transferor.

The effect of an ETIP is that, although GST exemption is allocable during the ETIP, the allocation is not effective before the ETIP ends. This rule does not apply to property for which a reverse QTIP election is made according to Code Section 2652(a)(3).[35]

---

[32]Code § 2642(f).

[33]Code § 2642(f)(4).

[34]57 Fed. Reg. 61363 (1992).

[35]Prop. Treas. Reg. § 26.2632-1(c)(1), 57 Fed. Reg. 61363 (1992).

For purposes of determining the occurrence of an ETIP, the transferor generally is deemed to possess any interest (or, apparently, any power and any other connection with the trust) that his or her spouse actually possesses.[36] This rule applies "only to the extent the spouse acquired the interest from the transferor in an inter vivos transfer that was not included in the transferor's taxable gifts or for which a [marital] deduction was allowed [for gift tax purposes]."[37] Although the Code does support clauses (i) and (iii) of Section 26.2632-1(c)(2) of the proposed regulations, this writer is unable to find any support in the Code for the attribution rule in clause (ii).

Although the preamble to the proposed regulations explicitly treats a power (that is, a power to establish or alter beneficial enjoyment of the trust) the same as an interest (that is, a right or a possibility to receive income or principal from the trust), the proposed regulations mention only an "interest" and not a "power." Nevertheless, this writer is informed that "interest" is intended to include "power." If "interest" does include "power," it probably also includes any other connection that the transferor's spouse has with the trust. A connection that is neither an interest nor a power has significance for purposes of Code Section 2042(2).[38]

According to the proposed regulations, if the ETIP occurs because of something that would cause inclusion in the gross estate of the transferor's spouse or, because of attribution from the spouse to the transferor, in the gross estate of the transferor, the ETIP ends no later than "the time at which no portion of the property would be includable in the spouse's gross estate (other than by reason of section 2035)." According to this formulation, unless the spouse's connection with the property would cause inclusion in the spouse's gross estate, the ETIP ends as soon as it begins. This writer understands that the Internal Revenue Service is rethinking this provision.

Any transfer that is a direct skip is treated as a direct skip occurring at the time that an effective allocation of GST exemp-

---

[36] Prop. Treas. Reg. § 26.2632-1(c)(2)(ii), 57 Fed. Reg. 61363 (1992).

[37] *Id.*

[38] See § 6.09, *infra*

tion first is permitted. The value of the property is its value for estate tax purposes or, if the property is not includable in the transferor's gross estate, its value at the time that an effective allocation of GST exemption first is permitted.[39]

§ 5.06 INCOME TAX ADJUSTMENTS BECAUSE OF THE GENERATION-SKIPPING TAX

§ 5.06(a) Sale or Exchange Treatment

If corporate stock is included in a generation-skipping transfer that occurs at the same time as, and because of, the death of an individual, sale or exchange (rather than dividend) treatment according to Code Section 303 is available as if (i) the individual owned the subject of the transfer (including the corporate stock) and no other property and (ii) the generation-skipping tax were the estate tax.[40]

§ 5.06(b) Basis Adjustments

If the generation-skipping transfer does not occur at the same time as, and because of, the death of an individual, the basis of the transferred property shall be increased (but not in excess of fair market value) by an amount equal to the generation-skipping tax attributable to any excess of value over basis.[41] If the transfer occurs at the same time as, and because of, the death of an individual, the basis of the property shall be adjusted in a manner similar to that provided by Code Section 1014; provided, if the inclusion ratio is less than one, any increase or decrease in basis shall not exceed the percentage of the total that is equal to the inclusion ratio.[42]

§ 5.06(c) Income in Respect of a Decedent

When income in the nature of income in respect of a decedent is subject to generation-skipping tax because of a taxable termination or a direct skip that occurs because of the death of the trans-

[39]Code § 2642(f).

[40]Code § 303(d).

[41]Code § 2654(a)(1).

[42]Code § 2654(a)(2).

feror, a deduction is available for income tax purposes for the generation-skipping tax that is attributable to the income.[43]

§ 5.06(d) Deduction for Income Distribution

A deduction is available for income tax purposes for the generation-skipping tax that is attributable to an income distribution that is included in the distributee's gross income but to which the throwback rules do not apply.[44]

---

[43]Code § 691(c)(3).

[44]Code § 164.

6

Application to Particular Formats

§ 6.01 OVERALL ANALYSIS

This chapter analyses how the generation-skipping tax applies to selected formats. It builds upon the statement of the law that precedes it, and it is a foundation for the analysis of planning that follows. Each format that is analyzed is included because it is commonly used or is particularly instructive. Generally, a discussion of planning implications, even those that inhere in formats analyzed in this chapter, is deferred to the following Chapters 7 and 8.

§ 6.02 PROVISION FOR PAYMENT OF TAX

Unless the governing instrument directs otherwise by specific reference to the tax imposed by Chapter 13, the generation-skipping tax shall be charged to the property constituting the generation-skipping transfer.[1] Governing instruments commonly have provided for payment of taxes payable "because of the testator's [settlor's] death." Many of these instruments do not mention the generation-skipping tax specifically. Others mention it specifically but only in the obsolete context of directing the fiduciary not to pay it with respect to transfers of which the testator or settlor is the deemed transferor. Code Section 2603(b) purports to state a federal rule of construction. It might avoid a construction issue when the governing instrument is silent about the generation-skipping tax or contains an obsolete direction against payment. It appar-

[1]Code § 2603(b).

ently permits retention of some pre-TRA '86 documents that, but for the rule, would require only a new tax clause.

A property owner who wants to leave shares that are equal (or shares that otherwise bear a fixed relationship to each other), regardless of whether any share attracts liability for generation-skipping tax, or who wants to leave a gross amount (rather than a gross amount minus generation-skipping tax attributable to the amount), must avoid the general rule and thus affirmatively must cause the instrument to provide for payment from another source. See Appendix Form #9, *infra.* The most common examples are per stirpital gifts that cannot qualify for the predeceased child exception, because the gifts either are not in the format of a direct skip or are to descendants of a person other than the property owner and other than the property owner's spouse or former spouse. Another common example is a gift of a number of shares or dollars to an unrelated employee who is the age of the transferor and a gift of the same or another number of shares or dollars to another employee, also unrelated, who is 38 years younger than the transferor. Another example is a gift of a particular number of shares or dollars to a brother's child and a gift of the same or another number of shares or dollars to the only living child of the brother's deceased child.

§ 6.03 EFFECT OF THE TRUSTEE'S EXERCISE OF DISCRETION TO PAY OBLIGATIONS OF THE EXECUTOR AND OF THE MERE POWER TO MAKE THESE PAYMENTS

What are the implications of a trustee of a trust ("Trust Number 1"), included in the transferor's gross estate, having discretion to discharge, at other than arms' length, charges against the grantor's estate? The mere existence of discretion in the trustee to distribute trust property to the transferor's estate other than at arms' length is capable of increasing the exposure of the trust estate to generation-skipping tax. The mere existence of the discretion causes the transferor's personal representative to be a permissible recipient of property of the trust and, therefore, for generation-skipping tax purposes, a holder of an "interest" in it.[2]

[2]Code § 2652(c).

According to Code Section 2651(e)(2),

> each individual having a beneficial interest in [Trust Number 1 through the estate or, if the estate is a permissible recipient of property from an intermediary trust that in turn is a permissible recipient of property from Trust Number 1, through the estate by way of the intermediary trust,] shall be treated as having an interest in [the trust estate of Trust Number 1]. . . .

Any individual, then, who has an interest that the exercise of the described discretion of the trustee of Trust Number 1 can enhance has an interest in the trust estate of Trust Number 1. To the extent that discretionary distributions from Trust Number 1 to the transferor's estate discharge what otherwise would be charges against a particular individual's interest in the estate and, therefore, increase the property this individual receives from the estate, the distributions constitute distributions to this individual. To the extent the discretionary distributions do not first exhaust the trustee's discretion, a termination of this person's interest in Trust Number 1 occurs when the transferor's estate ceases to be a permissible distributee of Trust Number 1. Whether the distributions are generation-skipping transfers in the form of taxable distributions or a taxable termination and whether the termination is a generation-skipping transfer in the form of a taxable termination should be determined precisely the same as whether for generation-skipping tax purposes any distribution in any other context is a taxable distribution or a taxable termination and whether for generation-skipping tax purposes any termination of an interest in any other context is a taxable termination.

The planner must realize that investing the trustee of Trust Number 1 with discretion to distribute trust property directly or indirectly to the transferor's estate other than at arms' length can have generation-skipping tax implications. The planner must analyze these implications each time he or she considers installing the discretion. Nevertheless, neither the installation nor the exercise of the discretion *inherently* increases exposure to generation-skipping tax.

An example (as regards a taxable distribution) of when the installation and exercise of the described discretion can generate exposure to *additional* generation-skipping tax occurs when property from Trust Number 1 is *distributed* directly or indirectly to the transferor's estate with the effect (to the extent of the distribution) of discharging estate charges otherwise chargeable against the interest of any person who is (or a trust all the persons who have present interests in which are) assigned to a generation that is at least two lower than the generation to which the transferor is assigned. An example (as regards a taxable termination) of when the installation of the discretion can generate exposure to *additional* generation-skipping tax occurs when any property of Trust Number 1 is *distributable* directly or indirectly to the transferor's estate with the effect (if and to the extent so distributed) of discharging estate charges otherwise chargeable against the interest of any skip person who is in the second generation below the transferor and Trust Number 1, but for the described discretion, is for the sole benefit of skip persons in the third generation below the transferor.

The first configuration described in the preceding paragraph can occur when Trust Number 1, but for the described discretion, is a discretionary trust for the sole benefit of the transferor's children and all or a portion of the transferor's residuary probate estate passes outright to the transferor's grandchildren. The second configuration described in the preceding paragraph can occur when (i) after the transferor's death Trust Number 1, but for the described discretion, is to pass outright to the transferor's great-grandchildren, and (ii) all or a portion of the transferor's residuary probate estate passes outright to the transferor's grandchildren.

While neither the first nor the second configuration is inherently imprudent in a dispositive sense, perhaps the transferor more generally will want to make similar or identical the dispositive schemes of (i) the portion of his or her estate that he or she charges with payment of death costs and (ii) Trust Number 1. Typically, for example, the portion of the transferor's estate that is charged with payment of death costs will either "pour over" to a trust established by the transferor during his or her life (for example, Trust Number 1 or a trust that is dispositively identical to Trust Number 1) or pass according to the transferor's will to a trust established under the will (for example, Trust Number 1 or a trust that is dispositively identical to Trust Number 1). When two trusts are dispositively identical, the ability of the trustee of either or each to make distributions to the trustee of the other should not enlarge whatever exposure to generation-skipping tax would inhere in each trust separately if neither were a permissible distributee of the other.

The passage of property from one trust to an identical trust (directly or through the medium of the transferor's estate) should not constitute a taxable distribution or a taxable termination, and the termination of the ability of one identical trust to be a permissible recipient (directly or through the medium of the transferor's estate) of property from the other should not constitute a taxable termination. The two trusts should present precisely the same vulnerability to generation-skipping tax as if they were one.

§ 6.04 CREDIT SHELTER TRUST

Assume the existence of a nonmarital trust — perhaps a credit shelter trust — for the benefit of the grantor's spouse (or the grantor's spouse and descendants) until the death of the grantor's spouse, remainder outright to the descendants, per stirpes, of the grantor who survive the survivor of the grantor and the grantor's spouse. The grantor is the transferor. During the life of the spouse, any distribution to a descendant other than a child (and that, according to the proposed regulations, does not terminate all interests of the spouse and the children in the trust) will be a taxable distribution. During the life of the spouse, according to the proposed regulations, any distribution that is to a descendant other than a child and that terminates all interests of the spouse and children in the trust is a taxable termination, even though the distribution is discretionary rather than mandatory. If upon the spouse's death any property passes to a descendant other than a child, the spouse's death will be a taxable termination.

§ 6.05 QTIP TRUST

Assume the existence of a QTIP trust for the benefit of the grantor's spouse until the death of the grantor's spouse, remainder to the descendants, per stirpes, of the grantor who survive the survivor of the grantor and the grantor's spouse.

§ 6.05(a) Determination of the Transferor

By means of an election, or a failure to make an election, according to Code Section 2652(a)(3), to ignore the QTIP election for generation-skipping tax purposes, the grantor (or the grantor's executor) can determine whether the grantor or the grantor's spouse is the transferor. An election causes the grantor to be the transferor. A failure to elect causes the grantor's spouse to be the transferor.

§ 6.05(b) Resulting Determinations

Since the election determines the identity of the transferor, it also determines

1. The generation assignments of individuals and whether a transfer to a particular individual, or the termination of the interest of a particular individual, is a generation-skipping transfer;
2. Whether a generation-skipping transfer upon the death of the grantor's surviving spouse is a taxable termination or, on the other hand, is a direct skip (or, if to a child of a deceased child of the transferor or of the transferor's spouse or former spouse, is not a generation-skipping transfer); and
3. The inclusion ratio.

If the spouse of the grantor is the transferor, the transfer upon the death of the spouse of any property to a descendant other than a child and other than a child of a deceased child of the transferor (or of the transferor's spouse or former spouse, that is, the grantor) will be a direct skip. If the spouse of the grantor is the transferor, the transfer upon the death of the spouse of any property to a child of a deceased child of the transferor (or of the transferor's spouse or former spouse, that is, the grantor) will be treated as if it were a transfer to a child of the transferor and hence will not be a direct skip and will not be a generation-skipping transfer. If the grantor is the transferor, the transfer upon the death of the spouse of the grantor of any property to a descendant other than a child will be a taxable termination.

§ 6.06 SINGLE "FAMILY" TRUST FOR ALL CHILDREN (OR DESCENDANTS) VERSUS SEPARATE TRUST FOR EACH CHILD (OR EACH CHILD AND THE CHILD'S DESCENDANTS)

§ 6.06(a) The Different Formats

Often, a person who has relatively modest wealth will want to make all of it available for any child who might have special needs. The owner might worry that a separate share established immediately upon his or her death, or upon the death of his or her surviving spouse, for each living child and for the descendants collectively of each deceased child will disadvantage the younger child(ren) if the owner or his or her spouse provided certain items (for example, education or automobiles) for the older, but not the younger, child(ren). This client often uses a single "family" trust for all of the children until no living child is less than a stated age (perhaps 21), with or without a child of a deceased child to be a permissible distributee upon the death of the parent, rather than separate shares in trust, one for each child.

§ 6.06(b) The Different Results

The single trust format offers a potential advantage, compared to the separate trust format, concerning the time of imposition of the generation-skipping tax. If the separate trust format is used and, therefore, the death of a child causes property to pass to, or for the benefit of, one or more of the child's descendants, the child's death will be a taxable termination. If the single trust format is used and a deceased child is survived by a sibling, no taxable termination will occur until the termination of the last interest of a sibling in the property that will pass to the deceased child's descendants. This will occur no later than when the single trust terminates. If the single trust format provides that the descendants of a deceased child shall be permissible distributees during the continuance of the single trust, any distribution to a descendant of a deceased child during the life of a sibling of a deceased child will be a taxable distribution. If the single trust format provides that the pro rata portion of a child shall "peel off" from the single trust upon the death of the child and then pass to or for the descendants of the deceased child, the single trust effectively will shift to a hybrid format, with characteristics of both a single trust and separate trusts, and the child's death will be a taxable termination with respect to the peeled-off portion.[3]

§ 6.07 NONGENERAL POWERS OF APPOINTMENT

§ 6.07(a) In General

A nongeneral power of a donee to appoint trust property can create results for generation-skipping tax purposes that are similar to those that a discretionary power of a trustee to distribute trust property can create. The similarity exists because each type of power creates an interest in each person to whom the power holder presently can distribute, or cause distribution of, trust property. Depending upon the configuration of the trust, the termination of the interest can produce a taxable termination, and any exercise of the power can produce a taxable distribution or a taxable termination, that would not occur if the interest did not exist. These issues with respect to nongeneral powers are material if a nongeneral power is exercisable in favor of a person who has an interest only because the person is a permissible appointee. Whereas before the advent of the generation-skipping tax the grantor could have granted interests to persons to whom the grantor might have anticipated that the power holder would not distribute any property, the creation of this type of an interest after the advent of the generation-skipping tax can precipitate a very significant tax.

Given the similarity between the power of a trustee to distribute and the nongeneral power of a donee to appoint and given that the implications for generation-skipping tax purposes of the power of the trustee to distribute appear to be understood better than those of the power of the donee to appoint, this analysis uses and compares a model of each.

§ 6.07(b) "Trustee's Spray-Power Model"

The first model illustrates the discretionary power of the trustee to distribute income and principal ("Trustee's Spray-Power Model").

---

[3]Code § 2612(a)(2).

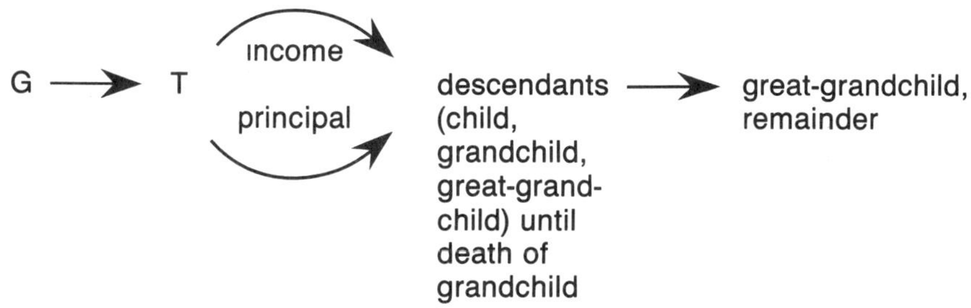

Assume that a property owner creates a trust to permit the trustee to pay income and principal to any one or more of the grantor's descendants (including the grantor's child, grandchild, and great-grandchild) until the death of the grantor's grandchild and to require the trustee to distribute any of the trust estate remaining at the death of the grandchild to the grandchild's descendants then living, per stirpes, or, if none, to the then-living descendants, per stirpes, of the grandchild's nearest ancestor who is the grantor or a child of the grantor and of whom one or more descendants then are living.

§ 6.07(c) "Donee's Nongeneral Power-of-Appointment Model"

The second model illustrates the nongeneral power of the donee to appoint principal ("Donee's Nongeneral Power-of-Appointment Model").

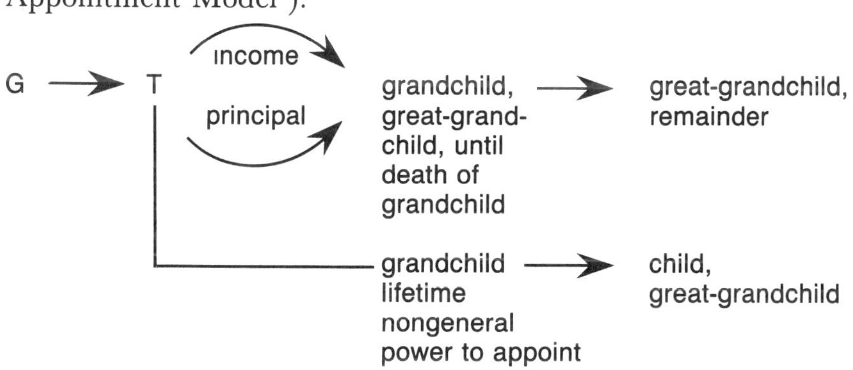

This model is identical to the Trustee's Spray-Power Model except that (i) the power of the trustee is not exercisable in favor of the child and (ii) the grandchild has a nongeneral power exercisable during life to appoint the principal to any one or more of the grantor's descendants (including the child but excluding the donee of the power).

§ 6.07(d) Discussion of the Models

§ 6.07(d)(1) Focus on the "Trustee's Spray Power Model"

First, focus upon the Trustee's Spray-Power Model.

§ 6.07(d)(1)(A) Distribution to the Great-Grandchild. A trustee's distribution of income or principal to the great-grandchild during the life of the grandchild, without (according to the proposed regulations) terminating all interest of each person who is assigned to a generation higher than great-grandchild, is a taxable distribution. Even if the distribution to the great-grandchild occurs during the life of the child and, therefore, skips two generations, it only is one generation-skipping transfer. Although the distribution during the life of the child to a person other than the child inherently causes the child's interest in the distributed property to cease to exist, this cessation does not cause the distribution to be classified as a taxable termination. Stated differently, the distribution to the great-grandchild during the life of the child is not additionally a taxable termination or alternatively two taxable terminations. Any other analysis would cause the concept of a taxable termination to consume the concept of a taxable distribution except in rather esoteric configurations. See § 8.04, *infra.* This writer sometimes will use the term "Taxable Distribution Prototype" to describe the situation in which a distribution is a taxable distribution even though it inherently causes a person's interest in the distributed property, held in trust, to cease to exist.[4]

§ 6.07(d)(1)(B) Termination of Child's Interest Before the Death of the Grandchild. The termination of the child's interest because of the death of the child (or if, alternatively, the child's interest is designed to lapse upon the expiration of a period of time, the expiration of the period) before the death of the grandchild is a taxable termination.

§ 6.07(d)(1)(C) Termination of Grandchild's Interest After the Termination of the Child's Interest. If trust property passes to the great-grandchild because of the death of the grandchild after the death of the child, or other termination of the interest of the child, the death of the grandchild is another taxable termination.

---

[4]*See* Code § 2612(a)(1).

§ 6.07(d)(1)(D) Termination of Child's Interest Because of the Death of the Grandchild. However, if trust property passes to the great-grandchild upon the death of the grandchild and the child's interest ceases only because of the death of the grandchild, the question is the number of taxable events, one or two, that occur. The grandchild's death does not only terminate the grandchild's interest. It also requires distribution of all of the trust estate to the great-grandchild, and this distribution inherently causes the child to cease to be a permissible distributee. The concept of two transfers for purposes of the generation-skipping tax occurring at the same time was familiar in the pre-TRA '86 version of Chapter 13. According to the ordering rules used in the pre-TRA '86 version of Chapter 13, any tax attributable to a first taxable termination (for example, at the level of the child's generation) was subtractable from the tax base for purposes of determining any tax upon a second taxable termination (for example, at the level of the grandchild's generation).[5] However, the proposed regulations seem definitively to answer the question by finding that a single event cannot produce more than one transfer for purposes of the generation-skipping tax.[6]

§ 6.07(d)(2) Focus on the "Donee's Nongeneral Power-of-Appointment Model"

Focus, next, upon the Donee's Nongeneral Power-of-Appointment Model.

The analysis appears to be precisely the same as the analysis with respect to the Trustee's Spray-Power Model. The conclusion, unremarkable but instructive, is that a nongeneral power of appointment can present the same implications for generation-skipping tax purposes as a power of a trustee to distribute. The mere existence of a particularly configured example of either type of power can produce a taxable termination. The exercise of a particu-

---

[5] *See* Staff of the Joint Committee on Taxation, *General Explanation of the Tax Reform Act of 1976,* 94th Cong., 2d Sess. 567 (1976).

[6] Prop. Treas. Reg. § 26.2612-1(f), Ex. 9, 57 Fed. Reg. 61362 (1992).

larly configured example of either type of power can produce a taxable distribution. The planning strategies, too, seem similar.[7]

Next, consider whether a nongeneral power exercisable solely by will confers an interest upon the permissible distributees and thus produces issues similar to those that the nongeneral, *inter vivos* power produces. Modification of the model merely by transforming the power of the grandchild into a testamentary power causes the child to have only a future interest, causes only skip persons to have interests when the trust is created and, therefore, causes the creation of the trust to be a direct skip. Therefore, the Donee's Nongeneral Power-of-Appointment Model requires additional modification if it is to illustrate a comparison of the two powers.

Start the comparison by assuming, as a variation of the Donee's Nongeneral Power-of-Appointment Model, that (i) the trustee is required to accumulate income and not distribute principal until two years after the trust is created, (ii) the nongeneral power of the grandchild to appoint commences two years after the trust is created, and (iii) the nongeneral power of the grandchild is not exercisable in favor of any person assigned to any generation higher than his or her own.

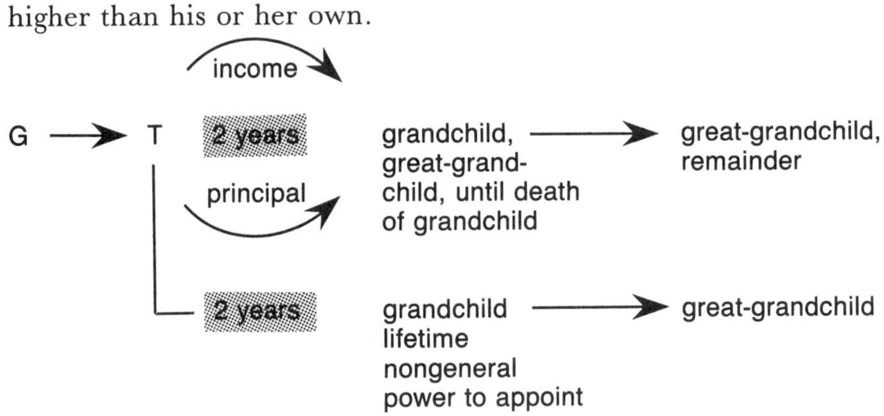

No person has an interest in the trust when the trust is created, and trust property can pass to a non-skip person upon termination of the trust. Therefore, arguably, the transfer that creates the trust is not to a skip person and thus is not a direct skip or a taxable distribution and is not a generation-skipping transfer.[8] This varia-

[7]See § 8.03, *infra.*

[8]See the discussion at § 8.04(b), *infra.*

tion of the Donee's Nongeneral Power-of-Appointment Model purposely is constructed so that, although no non-skip person has any interest, the property is not exempt from the generation-skipping tax and was not previously the subject of a generation-skipping transfer at the level of the child's generation (that is, the generation one below the grantor and one above the grandchild).

The modified Donee's Nongeneral Power-of-Appointment Model shows that the elimination of all interest of the child can reduce the transfer-tax cost of moving property to skip persons more than two generations below the transferor. Since no child has an interest before the death of the grandchild, the death of the child during the life of the grandchild is not a taxable termination. If trust property passes to the great-grandchild during the life of the grandchild, the passage is a generation-skipping transfer. According to the proposed regulations, the transfer is a taxable distribution if the grandchild has acquired an interest and the distribution does not terminate all of it, or it is a taxable termination if the grandchild has acquired an interest and the distribution does terminate all of it. If trust property passes to the great-grandchild upon the death of the grandchild within two years after the creation of the trust, the passage is a taxable distribution. If trust property passes to the great-grandchild upon the death of the grandchild more than two years after the creation of the trust, the death of the grandchild is a taxable termination. Even though the passage is to the great-grandchild and, therefore, skips two generations (that is, the generations that are the first and second below the transferor), only one generation-skipping transfer occurs. The conclusion is that the modifications of the Donee's Nongeneral Power-of-Appointment Model, including the removal of the interest in the child during the life of the grandchild, remove the possibility that movement of the property to a great-grandchild will require two taxable terminations rather than only one.

Next, complete the comparison by determining whether the addition of a nongeneral power exercisable solely by will in favor of the child undermines the reduction of generation-skipping transfers that elimination of all interest of the child can produce. Assume, as a variation of the modified version of the Donee's Nongeneral Power-of-Appointment Model, that (i) the nongeneral power of appointment of the grandchild is exercisable only by will and (ii) the child is not excluded as a permissible appointee.

Until the death of the donee, the power to appoint by will clearly is a future power, and the interests it confers clearly are future interests and hence not "interests" for purposes of the generation-skipping tax. However, does the power become a present power and, correspondingly, do the corresponding future interests become present interests, upon the death of the power holder? If the answers are affirmative and the child survives the grandchild, the death of the grandchild both creates and terminates a present interest of the child. The analysis appears to be similar to that at § 6.07(d)(1)(D), *supra.*[9] However, since, as previously mentioned, the proposed regulations find that a single event (here, the death of the grandchild) cannot produce more than one transfer for purposes of the generation-skipping tax, the death of the grandchild produces only one generation-skipping transfer, notwithstanding that it causes a skip of two generations.[10]

§ 6.07(d)(3) Other Configurations

Last, consider other configurations that can present the issue. Regardless of whether these examples are dispositively sensible, they might be instructive.

If, for example, the transferor's spouse or child is an income beneficiary for life and also a donee of a nongeneral power to appoint during life to any one or more of the transferor's descendants (other than the donee of the power), the donee fails to exercise the power and the property passes upon the donee's death to the transferor's great-grandchild, will two taxable terminations occur, or only one? The termination of the donee's interest clearly is a taxable termination. Will the donee's nongeneral power cause a grandchild to have an interest that terminates when the spouse's or child's nongeneral power terminates? Is the answer any different if the nongeneral power is exercisable only by will? Whether or not

---

[9] *See generally* Staff of the Joint Committee on Taxation, *General Explanation of the Tax Reform Act of 1976,* 94th Cong., 2d Sess. 567 (1976). *Cf.* pre-TRA '86 Code § 2613(c)(2) and Prop. Treas. Reg. (withdrawn) § 26.2613-4(e), Ex. (2).

[10] Prop. Treas. Reg. § 26.2612-1(f), Ex. 9, 57 Fed. Reg. 61362 (1992).

these situations present identical issues and analyses, the proposed regulations seem to provide the same answer, that is, the death of the donee produces only one generation-skipping transfer.

§ 6.08 EFFECT OF POWER TO DISCHARGE LEGAL OBLIGATION OWED TO A SKIP PERSON BY A PERSON OTHER THAN THE PERSON SERVING AS FIDUCIARY

§ 6.08(a) In General

If a trustee or a custodian of a gift under the Uniform Gifts to Minors Act ("UGMA") or Uniform Transfers to Minors Act ("UTMA") can distribute property with the effect of discharging a legal obligation (for example, an obligation of support) of another person, who is not named or described as a permissible distributee, the person whose legal obligation the trustee or custodian may discharge seems to possess an "interest" in the property unless something in the definition of "interest" prevents this result.

If the person who is named or described as a permissible distributee is a skip person but the obligor is a non-skip person, the obligor's possession of an interest might prevent the *creation* of the arrangement from being a direct skip or, indeed, a generation-skipping transfer. The non-skip person's interest might defer the occurrence of a generation-skipping transfer. Any discretionary distribution to the person who is named or described as a permissible distributee, not in discharge of any legal obligation of the obligor, might be a taxable transfer. According to the proposed regulations, the transfer would be a taxable distribution if the distribution did not terminate all of the obligor's interest or a taxable termination if the distribution did terminate all of the obligor's interest. Any non-discretionary termination of the obligor's interest, for example, because of the obligor's death, the termination of the trust or the UGMA or the UTMA arrangement or the termination otherwise of the obligation, might be a taxable termination. This arrangement might generate unnecessary liability. A direct skip has a relatively smaller tax base than either a taxable distribution or a taxable termination. Additionally, the arrangement might have prevented qualification for the grandchild exclusion.[11]

[11] See the discussion in § 7.05, *infra*.

If both the person who is named or described as a permissible distributee and the obligor are skip persons but the obligor is assigned to a higher generation, the obligor's possession of an interest might not prevent the initial transfer from being a direct skip but might generate an unnecessary, additional generation-skipping transfer. As mentioned previously, any discretionary distribution to the person who is named or described as a distributee, not in discharge of any legal obligation of the obligor, might be a taxable distribution or, if it terminates all interest of the obligor, a taxable termination. Also as mentioned previously, the termination of the obligor's interest might be a taxable termination.

If the problem can exist, it can apply to any trust (including, for example, a Code Section 2503(c) present-interest trust) or UGMA or UTMA arrangement established for the sole benefit of one or more minors. The Internal Revenue Service has asserted that a custodian of a gift under the Uniform Gifts to Minors Act can use the property to discharge the legal obligation (for example, an obligation of support) owed by another to the minor. When a nondonor custodian who was the parent of the minor died during the custodianship, the Service asserted that the custodial property was included in the gross estate of the custodian because the custodian possessed a general power to appoint the custodial property. The supposed ability of a custodian to discharge a legal obligation of someone other than the minor has caused the Service to assert that a person whose obligation the custodian can discharge but who is not the custodian has an interest in the custodianship. The Service treated the custodianship as a generation-skipping trust equivalent.[12] As a matter of policy, the Service said that the asserted interest would become a present interest only if the custodian *in fact* discharged an obligation of the person other than the minor and that it would not be a present interest if the custodian merely had the unexercised ability to do so.[13] In any other context, of course, if trust or trust equivalent property presently *could* be used to dis-

[12]Former Prop. Treas. Reg. (withdrawn because of repeal of first version of Chapter 13) § 26.2613-4(d).

[13]Former Prop. Treas. Reg. (withdrawn because of repeal of first version of Chapter 13) § 26.2613-4(e), Ex. (3).

charge the obligation, the obligor would have an "interest" without regard to whether the property in fact was used for that purpose.

§ 6.08(b) A Drafting Solution to the Problem

If the transfer is in trust, the draftsperson can eliminate the issue by explicitly precluding use of trust property to discharge any legal obligation owed by a person who is not named or described as a permissible distributee.[14] This type of drafting appears impossible for an UGMA or UTMA gift.

§ 6.08(c) A Statutory Solution to the Problem

Code Section 2652(c) provides a statutory solution to most manifestations of the problem. Unless the trust expressly requires the described distributions, the mere possibility of the described distributions is to be disregarded for purposes of determining whether a person has an "interest." The provision seems unclear about whether the actual, discretionary use of the property for this purpose will cause the person whose legal obligation is thus discharged to have an interest. However, according to the proposed regulations, a person does not have an interest if the property is usable to satisfy the person's legal obligation only within the discretion of a fiduciary or according to the Uniform Transfers to Minors Act or the Uniform Gifts to Minors Act.[15] This rule is of questionable validity to the extent that avoidance of an interest requires that a *fiduciary* possess the discretion. The Code does not include the requirement that a fiduciary possess the discretion. The rule of the proposed regulations would seem, for example, to cause a person to have an interest solely because another person, who is not a fiduciary, possesses a nongeneral power of appointment that the donee of the power can exercise to discharge the obligation of support of the first person.

§ 6.08(d) Apparent Exaggeration of the Problem

The problem seems very unlikely, in any event, in two contexts in which the Internal Revenue Service often asserts that it exists.

---

[14] See, for example, the language at § 7.05, *infra*.

[15] Prop. Treas. Reg. § 26.2612-1(e)(2), 57 Fed. Reg. 61361 (1992).

First, consider a trust in which the governing instrument does not explicitly permit payments for the support of any person who is named or described as a permissible distributee. In this context, distribution of trust property in discharge of the legal obligation of a person who is not named or described as a permissible distributee to support a person who is named or described as a permissible distributee would seem to be solely for the benefit of someone who is not named or described as a beneficiary. Therefore, the distribution would appear to violate the trust.

Second, consider a trust that explicitly does permit distributions for the health, education, and support of a named or described distributee, considering resources otherwise available to the named or described distributee. The obligation of another person to support the person who is named or described as a permissible distributee will be "resources otherwise available." Thus, the support obligation will preclude distributions from the trust.

§ 6.09 IRREVOCABLE INSURANCE TRUST

Assume the existence of an irrevocable insurance trust that upon the death of the insured grantor is to be distributed outright to, or held in continuing trust for, the grantor's descendants. The principal purposes of this trust are to remove the insurance proceeds from the gross estate of the insured, to minimize gift tax with respect to the insured's gifts of the premiums, to avoid subjecting the trust property to transfer tax *before* the insured dies, and to avoid subjecting the proceeds unnecessarily to transfer tax when the insured dies.

The grantor annually pays to the trustee the amount of the premiums. In order to reduce the amount of these gifts that will be subject to gift tax, the grantor attempts to qualify the gifts within the Code Section 2503(b) annual exclusion from taxable gifts for gifts of present interests, but the grantor generally desires to do this in such a manner as avoids including the gift property in the taxable gifts or gross estate of the donee. The grantor might accommodate these two objectives by giving the grantor's spouse and certain of the grantor's descendants rights to withdraw the gifts from the trust and by providing that the rights to withdraw shall expire as soon as they can expire consistently with both the contributions to the trust being present interest gifts and no release of a general power of appointment occurring for United States gift tax or estate tax purposes upon lapse of a right to withdraw.[16] Additionally, to inject some flexibility, the grantor might want to allow an independent trustee during the grantor's life to distribute trust property (and perhaps thereby to terminate the trust) to one or more persons.

§ 6.09(a) Pre-TRA '86 Generation-Skipping Tax

While the pre-TRA '86 version of Chapter 13 was in effect, the grantor had to evaluate whether installing a present interest in a child during the grantor's life warranted the risk of a generation-skipping tax during the grantor's life or upon the grantor's death. If the grantor's child had a present interest and died during the grantor's life and the subject property passed outright upon the grantor's death to the child's then-living descendants, per stirpes, the child's interest would have caused a taxable termination to occur with respect to the subject property no later (and perhaps sooner) than upon the grantor's death. If, on the other hand, no child had any present interest during the grantor's life and the property passed to children of a deceased child upon the grantor's death, no generation-skipping transfer would have occurred during the grantor's life or upon the grantor's death. Additionally, since all property that is subject to satisfying an interest is the subject of any generation-skipping transfer in the form of a taxable termination of the interest and a right to withdraw need not apply to other than the contributions in order to exclude the contributions from taxable gifts, the grantor might have attempted to reduce the scope of any generation-skipping transfer by confining the rights to withdraw to the contributions (or portions of them) and permitting the trustee otherwise to distribute to any person during the grantor's life only the property that the person then or previously had a right to withdraw.

§ 6.09(b) Effect of TRA '86

TRA '86 generally enhanced the attractiveness of the described trust with respect to transfers before April 1, 1988. Since

[16] *See* Code §§ 2041(b)(2) and 2514(e).

any property that reached the trust by means of a nontaxable gift (that is, a gift that qualified for the annual exclusion from taxable gifts according to Code Section 2503(b), after allowing for gift-splitting according to Code Section 2513(a)) was exemptible from the generation-skipping tax, *Crummey* powers[17] that excluded the subject property from the taxable gifts of the donor and that did not include it in the taxable gifts or gross estate of any donee could have exempted it as well from the generation-skipping tax.[18] Many irrevocable insurance trusts are designed to exclude all contributions from the taxable gifts of the donor and also from taxable gifts of each donee and, except to such extent as any right to withdraw must exist at the donee's death because any earlier lapse would produce a gift, gross estate of the donee. These trusts effectively also could be exempt from the generation-skipping tax without any allocation of GST exemption.

§ 6.09(c) Gifts After March 31, 1988

Effective with respect to transfers after March 31, 1988, the exemption is not available for any gift to a trust unless the trust property (i) is not distributable to any person other than the donee during the life of the donee and (ii) is includable in the gross estate of the donee for estate tax purposes if the donee dies before the trust terminates.[19]

If the described trust is not fully exempt from the generation-skipping tax, a generation-skipping transfer can occur during the grantor's life or upon the grantor's death *even if* no child has any present interest during the grantor's life. First, assume that the trust is not fully exempt because the grantor transfers a nonexempt gift, that is, a gift of a future interest or a gift which does not conform to the criteria for exemption of a nontaxable gift. Notwithstanding that the nonexempt gift is a gift which is considered to be a gift of a future interest for gift tax purposes, it might or might not cause an individual immediately to have an interest for generation-skipping tax

---

[17] *See* Crummey v. Commissioner, 397 F.2d 82 (9th Cir. 1968). See also §§ 7.03(a) and 7.03(b)(3), *infra*.

[18] Code § 2642(c).

[19] *Id.*

purposes. If any skip person has an interest immediately after the grantor makes the nonexempt gift but no non-skip person then has an interest, the nonexempt gift will be a generation-skipping transfer in the form of a direct skip. If any non-skip person has an interest immediately after the grantor makes the nonexempt gift, or if no person has an interest immediately after the grantor makes the nonexempt gift and a distribution may be made to a non-skip person later, no generation-skipping transfer will occur when the grantor makes the gift, but a generation-skipping transfer can occur later, in the form of a taxable termination or a taxable distribution. If no individual has an interest immediately after the grantor makes the nonexempt gift and at any time during the grantor's life but a distribution thereafter may be made to a non-skip person, no generation-skipping transfer will occur during the grantor's life, but a generation-skipping transfer will occur upon the grantor's death to such extent as property then is distributed to a grandchild or any other skip person.[20] The passage upon the grantor's death will not involve the termination of any interest and, therefore, will not involve a taxable termination.[21] If a non-skip person (for example, a child) who has an interest dies during the grantor's life and no non-skip person has an interest immediately after the death of the non-skip person but either a skip person then has an interest or a distribution thereafter may be made to a skip person, a taxable termination will occur upon the death of the non-skip person (that is, the child).[22]

Alternatively, assume that the trust is not fully exempt because a child of the grantor allows the lapse of a right to withdraw to be a transfer for gift tax or estate tax purposes (that is, not a nontaxable gift).[23] The child's transfer will cause the child to supplant the grantor as the transferor.[24] Thus, with respect to this transfer, the grantor's grandchildren will become non-skip persons. Although this transfer might undermine the trust's exemption from

[20]Code § 2612(b).

[21]Code § 2612(a)(1).

[22]Code § 2612(a).

[23]*See* Code § 2041.

[24]Code § 2652(a).

the generation-skipping tax, the undermining effectively might occur only at the level of transfers from grandchildren and descendants assigned to yet lower generations.

If the trust (including the insurance proceeds) is subject to inclusion in the gross estate of the insured only if the insured dies within three years after transferring a policy on his or her life to the trustee, the transferor's allocation of GST exemption is effective even before the three-year period expires.[25] Accordingly, whether or not the insured survives the three-year-period, the increase in value that results when the insured dies does not change the inclusion ratio that applied before the insured died.[26] However, if the trust is subject to inclusion in the gross estate of the insured for any other reason, an ETIP exists, and the allocation of GST exemption to the trust is not effective until the ETIP ends. The transferor's nontaxable gift to his or her spouse by means of a *Crummey* power creates an ETIP, both because of the attribution rule discussed at § 5.05(e), *supra,* and because the property that is subject to the *Crummey* power is includable in the gross estate of the spouse if the spouse dies while possessing the power.[27]

Consider whether an ETIP occurs if a transferor transfers property to his or her spouse as trustee and grants to the spouse

(i) a present right as trustee to manage (but not distribute) the property,

(ii) a *Crummey* power and

(iii) a nongeneral power of appointment exercisable during life before the death of the transferor

and, *in the future,* during the spouse's life after the death of the transferor,

(iv) a power to distribute the principal to such appointees as the spouse directs by means of a nongeneral power of appointment and

(v) a power to pay principal to the spouse for his or her health, education, and support

---

[25] *See* Code § 2642(f).

[26] Prop. Treas. Reg. § 26.2642-4(a)(3), 57 Fed. Reg. 61367 (1992).

[27] *See* Prop. Treas. Reg. § 26.2632-1(c)(2)(iii), 57 Fed. Reg. 61363 (1992).

and, upon the death of the transferor's spouse after the death of the transferor,

(vi) a power to distribute the property as the spouse directs by will by means of a nongeneral power of appointment.

Among the listed powers, interests, and other connections, the *Crummey* power is unique. As previously mentioned, it produces an ETIP even without any attribution from the spouse to the transferor. If an ETIP occurs because the transferor's spouse possesses any of the other interests, powers, and connections, it occurs solely because of the attribution rule.

If the transferor held the spouse's nongeneral power exercisable during the transferor's life, the power would cause inclusion in the transferor's gross estate according to Code Sections 2036(a)(2) and 2038(a)(1).

If attributed to the transferor, the service of the transferor's spouse as trustee, *per se,* would seem to cause the transferor to possess an incident of ownership in a policy of insurance on the life of the transferor and, therefore, cause inclusion in the gross estate of the transferor according to Code Section 2042(2).[28]

The other powers and interests listed above become "present" powers and interests only after the transferor dies. Therefore, even if a means is found to attribute to the transferor something that does not exist before the transferor is deceased or to attribute something to the transferor after the transferor is deceased, it is difficult to understand how they can rise to the dignity of being described in Code Section 2036 or Code Section 2038.

Even assuming that powers and other connections of the transferor's spouse are attributable to the transferor the same as interests (see § 5.05(e), *supra*), no attribution occurs unless "the spouse acquired the interest [or power or other connection] from

[28]*See* Horn, *Fiduciary-Insured's Incidents of Ownership: An Analysis of Recent Cases,* 3 EST. PLAN. 66 (Winter, 1976), and the discussion of Estate of Fruehauf v. Commissioner, 427 F.2d 80 (6th Cir. 1970); Estate of Skifter v. Commissioner, 468 F.2d 699 (2d Cir. 1972); Rose v. United States, 511 F.2d 259 (5th Cir. 1975); and Terriberry v. United States, 517 F.2d 286 (5th Cir. 1975). *Cf.* Rev. Rule. 84-179, 84-2 C.B. 195; Hunter v. United States, 624 F.2d 833 (8th Cir. 1980); and Estate of Bloch v. Commissioner, 78 T.C. 850 (1982).

the transferor in an inter vivos transfer that was not included in the transferor's taxable gifts or for which a [marital] deduction was allowed [for gift tax purposes]."[29] However, even if the transferor does not give to his or her spouse any gift that qualifies for an annual exclusion or the marital deduction, the spouse often does receive his or her interests, powers, and other connections by means of inter vivos transfers that are "not included in the transferor's taxable gifts." Stated differently, the quoted language seems sufficiently broad to subject the spouse's interests, powers, and other connections to the test of attribution.

[29]Prop. Treas. Reg. § 26.2632-1(c)(2)(ii), 57 Fed. Reg. 61363 (1992).

7

Strategies To Reduce or Avoid the Tax — Part I (Planning for Favored Property and Transfers)

§ 7.01 THE OVERRIDING PRINCIPLES

Two overriding principles and a corollary govern the reduction or avoidance of the generation-skipping tax.

§ 7.01(a) Use the Four Preferences

First, use optimally the various preferences. They are

1. The GST exemption,
2. The annual exclusion,
3. The qualified transfer, and
4. The predeceased child exception.

These preferences are listed in the order of what this writer considers to be their relative importance. Although maximization of generation-skipping transfers for the purpose of enhancing benefits from GST exemptions can conflict with nontax objectives, the GST exemption does not *require* this distortion. The GST exemption is universally available. As a practical matter, annual exclusion gifts are unavailable to many moderately wealthy families whose wealth, nevertheless, is sufficient to attract liability for generation-skipping tax. Qualified transfers are relatively modest. The availability of the predeceased child exception depends upon the occurrence of a fortuity — the death of a child before the death of a parent (or spouse or former spouse of a parent). Until 1990, the grandchild exclusion also was a preference. The grandchild exclusion was available only for a limited time. It was particularly capable of distorting the dispositive arrangement that a property owner would have created if the generation-skipping tax were not a factor.

§ 7.01(b) Avoid Unnecessary Generation-Skipping Transfers

Second, avoid any generation-skipping transfer that is neither necessary nor desirable. Any property owner has the absolute ability to avoid involvement with the generation-skipping tax. The cost, of course, is involvement instead with Chapter 12 (the gift tax) or Chapter 11 (the estate tax). Effectively, the ability entirely to avoid Chapter 13 is a preference. This writer purposely includes it last. This writer believes that the property owner (or the owner's surrogate) should defer, until after considering the availability of the other preferences and the complexion of beneficiaries' transfer tax bases at the time a generation-skipping tax is sought to be avoided, a decision actually to use (as opposed to permit the use of) this technique. The desirability of this deferred consideration suggests the use of techniques discussed in § 8.01, *infra.* Next in sequence, the planner should consider using the structure of Chapter 13, other than its preferences, to reduce or avoid generation-skipping transfers. See §§ 8.02, 8.03, and 8.04, *infra.*

§ 7.01(c) Preserve Flexibility

Third, the corollary: When possible, preserve flexibility.

The preferences are discussed in this chapter.

§ 7.02 USE OF THE GST EXEMPTION

§ 7.02(a) General Principles

§ 7.02(a)(1) The Overriding Principle — Maximize the Present Value

The Overriding Principle about allocating the GST exemption is to allocate it in such a manner as tends to maximize its present value. Maximization of the present value of the GST exemption means maximization of the present value of the property that the exemption can permit to inure to the benefit of the beneficiaries of the transferor (or of the transferor's spouse) rather than to the United States. The present value of the exemption is a function of the number and size of generation-skipping transfers to which the property might be subject if it is not exempt, discounted for probability and time of occurrence. The statutory mechanism for "default" allocation of the exemption to trusts from which a taxable termination or taxable distribution can occur ignores both probability and time of occurrence.

Five examples illustrate the concept of the present value of the GST exemption:

1. Even if a particular disposition can produce a generation-skipping transfer, diversions from skip persons, including distributions to non-skip persons, reduce the value of exempting the underlying property.
2. A trust for the life of a child, remainder to a grandchild, has a high probability of producing a generation-skipping transfer. However, the value of exempting the property is a function of discounting to present value a tax saving that, viewed actuarially, occurs only at the end of the child's life expectancy.
3. The value of exempting a direct skip, on the other hand, is a function of exempting a transfer that is certain to occur presently.
4. A trust that is to pass outright to a child at age 30 but that is to pass to a grandchild if the child dies before then can produce a generation-skipping transfer. However, the transfer is improbable. Therefore, the allocation of GST exemption to the property has a low value.
5. The value of exempting property that can qualify as QTIP is a function of the spouse's life expectancy, required distributions to the spouse (that is, a non-skip person), and the possibility of other diversions from skip persons. Income payments to the grantor's spouse are required. Principal payments to the grantor's spouse are optional but com-

mon. Payment of death costs upon the death of the grantor's spouse is common.

a. If the surviving spouse directs the payment of these costs from his or her own property rather than from fully exempt QTIP and thus exonerates the QTIP so that the QTIP does not pay the reimbursement described in Code Section 2207A, the QTIP remains fully exempt after the payment, and the payment from other property is not an addition which, to be exempt, requires allocation of the spouse's GST exemption.[1]

b. If the governing instrument imposes these costs upon a marital trust that is not exempt and thereby exonerates QTIP that is fully exempt, the QTIP remains fully exempt after the payment, and the payment that Code Section 2207A would require the QTIP to reimburse is not an addition that, to be exempt, requires allocation of the spouse's GST exemption.[2] The theory upon which this conclusion is based in each case is that (i) the right of reimbursement arises because of a QTIP election and (ii) a reverse QTIP election according to Code Section 2652(a)(3) treats the QTIP election as though, for generation-skipping tax purposes, it was not made.

The determination and comparison of present values of tax savings that are attributable to alternative allocations of GST exemption depend upon five factors.

First, other things being equal, the greater the value of the subject property each time tax is avoided, the greater the present value of the allocation. A higher rate of return on investment produces more value than a lower return. Diversions of the property from skip persons, consisting of distributions to, and consumption by, non-skip persons, reduce the value. Examples, in the case of life insurance, include (i) exhaustion of the risk portion, as a function of time, during the life of the insured and (ii)

---

[1] Prop. Treas. Reg. § 26.2652-1(a)(5), 57 Fed. Reg. 61368 (1992).

[2] *Id.*

termination of the insurance, because the insurer refuses to insure the risk, before the death of the insured.

Second, greater frequency of avoidance of taxable events tends to produce a greater saving than a lesser frequency. As an example, a trust that is designed to exist for the period of the Rule Against Perpetuities will tend to avoid more taxable events than a trust that must terminate upon the death of the grantor's child. The GST exemption can avoid generation-skipping tax during the entire period of the Rule Against Perpetuities. By contrast, nontaxable gifts (as, for example, (i) qualified transfers according to Code Section 2503(e), (ii) direct skips that are outright, and (iii) a direct skip to a Code Section 2642(c) trust) only can "avoid" one generation-skipping transfer.

Third, other things being equal, the passage of less time before a saving of tax produces a greater value than the passage of more.

Fourth, other things being equal, a higher probability of the occurrence of a taxable event tends to produce a greater saving than a lower probability.

Fifth, subtract the present value of the costs that the transferor incurs by making a lifetime gift in order to save generation-skipping tax but that the transferor could avoid by not making the gift. These costs include foregone enjoyment of the gift and of the gift tax. The analysis requires (i) a comparison of the present values of payment of less gift tax earlier with payment of more estate tax later and (ii) a determination of who bears the cost of a lifetime gift and of a deathtime transfer.

§ 7.02(a)(2) Efficient Allocation of the GST Exemption

Other things being equal, efficient implementation of the Overriding Principle requires allocation of the GST exemption in such a manner as completely exempts a fund of property rather than in such a manner as partially exempts a fund.

§ 7.02(a)(2)(A) The Purpose. The purpose is to promote efficient use of the exemption. The fiduciary can make nontaxable distributions to skip persons from a totally exempt fund. Correspondingly, the fiduciary can make nontaxable distributions to non-skip persons from a totally nonexempt fund. Distributions to

skip persons from a partially exempt, partially nonexempt fund are taxable transfers. Distributions to non-skip persons from a partially exempt, partially nonexempt fund waste some of the GST exemption.

This strategy requires either separate trusts or separate shares that are treated as separate trusts. Otherwise, fractional shares of a single trust are not treated as separate trusts with separate inclusion ratios. If the unallocated GST exemption of a transferor is insufficient completely to exempt all of the property that is subject to a particular disposition, the transferor must divide (or provide for another to divide) the disposition into two parts, one of which is sufficient to absorb the GST exemption and the other of which is the balance.

§ 7.02(a)(2)(B) The Techniques. Two types of techniques appear available to accomplish this result.

First, the transferor might transform substantively, and dispose separately, the portion that exceeds the unused GST exemption.

Second, the transferor might fractionalize (or permit another to fractionalize) a disposition into portions that are substantively identical or (if, for example, a feature, such as a general power of appointment, applies only to a nonexempt disposition) similar, one intended to be entirely exempt, the other intended to be entirely nonexempt.

One procedure of fractionalizing a dispostion into portions is to grant the fiduciary discretion to sever a single trust into separate trusts. Even if discretionary severance of a single fund into two portions, one totally exempt and the other totally nonexempt, were ineffective, the attempt would seem not to undermine any other planning. Drafting of permission for any discretionary severance probably should parallel drafting for severance of property that can qualify as QTIP into a marital portion and a nonmarital portion — that is, the severance should occur based upon fair market values at the time of the severance.[3] If the severance precedes, rather than follows, allocation of the transferor's GST exemption, the severance of a single fund should produce separate funds that

[3]*See* Prop. Treas. Reg. § 20.2056(b)-7(b), and Appendix, Form #1, *infra.*

after the severance and the application of GST exemption to one of them are, respectively, exempt and nonexempt.

A second procedure of fractionalizing a dispostion into portions is to provide that *if* any GST exemption remains unallocated after the transferor's executor otherwise allocates it, the trustee *shall* (not *may*) separate a single trust into two trusts, one consisting of such portion as can absorb the unallocated GST exemption and the other consisting of the balance. This formulation uses the language of a mandate. However, since the mandate is subject to a contingency that is a function of the exercise of discretion, this procedure appears no more mandatory than the first.

A third procedure is to require a division into shares, one share to consist of the portion that can absorb the unallocated GST exemption determined *before* the executor makes any discretionary allocation of it, the other to consist of the balance. This procedure can characterize both the first technique (that is, using dispositions that differ substantively depending upon whether they are exempt or nonexempt) and the second (that is, using fractional portions that are substantively identical or similar). Without more, this formulation appears to create a real mandate. However, if the governing instrument authorizes the discretionary consolidation of the identical trusts, the mandate might be more apparent than real. The mandatory system might create a share that exceeds the GST exemption that the executor in fact will agree to allocate. Inclusion of authority for a fiduciary, in its discretion, to sever a single trust into more than one trust according to the procedure previously described might permit the fiduciary to reduce the trust so that its size corresponds to the GST exemption that the executor will allocate. However, whether the trust will have an inclusion ratio of zero will depend on whether the severance is respected for purposes of the generation-skipping tax. Additionally, in any event, the "excess" trust that is nonexempt might have dispositive provisions that are better suited to an exempt trust.

No policy consideration should cause any one or more of these procedures to be any more or less availing than any one or more of the others. Nevertheless, in partial contravention of this principle, the division of a single trust into a wholly exempt trust and a parallel trust with a different inclusion ratio apparently requires the executor to allocate GST exemption after, rather than before, the division occurs. Additionally, the proposed regulations contravene this principle (i) entirely in some cases by precluding entirely the severance of any trust that is not included in the gross estate of the transferor and (ii) more than the statute in all other cases by espousing onerous procedures for effecting the split. Substantially separate and independent shares of different beneficiaries in a single trust, dating from the time of the transfer and existing because of the mandate of the trust, are severable at any time.[4] So, too, are shares that are attributable to different transferors to a single trust.[5] Otherwise, the severance of a single trust into separate trusts is recognized for purposes of the generation-skipping tax only if (i) the trust is included in the transferor's gross estate, (ii) the severance occurs before the due date for the estate tax return or the executor states on the estate tax return either the manner in which the fiduciary is accomplishing the severance according to authority in the governing instrument or that the fiduciary has begun a reformation proceeding to sever the trust according to state law, and (iii) the severance is made by means of fractional shares or, if the governing instrument requires the severance to be made on the basis of a pecuniary amount, the pecuniary amount is satisfied in a manner designed to assure that it receives neither more nor less than the values that the proposed regulations prescribe.[6] Except as noted, the proposed regulations apparently require aggregation of all trusts that would constitute a single trust if all severances were ignored.

§ 7.02(a)(3) Avoiding Commingling Property of Different Transferors

Other things being equal, a "transferor" and his or her executor should consider avoiding commingling any property with any property of which another person is the "transferor."

Distributions of nonexempt property to a particular person might produce, or not produce, a generation-skipping transfer,

---

[4]Prop. Treas. Reg. § 26.2654-1(b)(2), (c), 57 Fed. Reg. 61370-71 (1992).

[5]Prop. Treas. Reg. § 26.2654-1(b)(1), (c), 57 Fed. Reg. 61370-71 (1992).

[6]Prop. Treas. Reg. § 26.2654-1(c), 57 Fed. Reg. 61370 (1992).

depending upon whether one person, rather than another, is the transferor. Distributions of exempt property to a particular person might be necessary to avoid a generation-skipping transfer, or might waste GST exemption, depending upon whether one person, rather than another, is the transferor. The portions of a trust that are attributable to different transferors are treated as separate trusts.[7] However, if the governing instrument does not provide otherwise, the proposed regulations treat a distribution from a trust that has more than one transferor as being pro rata from each transferor. This pro rata treatment can produce the same effect as a distribution from a fund that is partially exempt and partially nonexempt and, therefore, can waste GST exemption and create unnecessary liability for the tax. These results might suggest providing for as many portions as permit each portion to have only one transferor.[8] If a single trust will or might include property of which different persons are transferors, the draftsperson at least should consider installing language that avoids the pro rata treatment that the regulations otherwise would require.[9]

§ 7.02(a)(4) Use of Principles That Affect the Potentially Exemptable Amount

Other things being equal, a transferor and the transferor's executor should use efficiently the principles that affect the amount that the GST exemption can exempt.

§ 7.02(a)(4)(A) Deferred Allocation. The rule that postpones allocation of GST exemption to property that would be includable in the transferor's gross estate immediately after the transfer has the apparent purpose of preventing the GST exemption from exempting any increase in value before the transfer of the underlying property is complete for gift tax and estate tax purposes.[10] However, the rule does not apply to the very case that most

---

[7]Code § 2654(b).

[8]*See* Appendix, Form #1, *infra.*

[9]*See* Appendix Form #11, *infra;* Prop. Treas. Reg. § 26.2654-1(a), 57 Treas. Reg. 61370 (1992).

[10]*See* Code § 2642(f).

presents the type of problem that precipitated the rule. It does not apply to insurance proceeds that are subject to inclusion in the insured's gross estate if the insured dies within three years after transferring the insurance, whether or not the insured survives the three-year period.[11]

§ 7.02(a)(4)(B) Charitable Lead Annuity Trusts. Since the rule that determines the applicable fraction, and, hence, the inclusion ratio, of a charitable lead annuity trust causes the applicable fraction to depend upon events that do not occur until after the exemption is allocated, the transferor or the transferor's executor must estimate the amount of GST exemption that is required to produce a given inclusion ratio and probably must allocate more than enough (and thus waste some) GST exemption in order to assure an inclusion ratio of zero.[12]

§ 7.02(a)(4)(C) Allocation of Appreciation and Depreciation. Allocation of appreciation and depreciation that has occurred between the transferor's death and the time of funding can waste GST exemption.[13]

If a trust or other disposition to which GST exemption is allocated is funded with property that does not include a ratable sharing of appreciation and depreciation in all property that is available for funding, values at dates of distribution (rather than values for estate tax purposes) shall control for purposes of allocation of GST exemption.

The apparent concern that underlies Code Section 2642(b)(2)(A) is that any disposition that is satisfiable at estate tax values with other than a ratable sharing of appreciation and depreciation permits skewing of value in favor of a generation-skipping arrangement that consists either of the disposition itself or of another disposition that is funded from the same pool of assets. The proposed regulations include complicated rules which are designed to address the concern of the Code and also a concern which is not clearly implicit in the Code, that delayed payment of a pecuniary legacy is capable, by itself, of skewing values.

---

[11] *See* Code § 2035(d)(2), and § 6.09, *supra.*

[12] *See* Code § 2642(e), and § 5.02(b)(2), *supra.*

[13] *See* Code § 2642(b)(2)(A), and Appendix, Form #4, *infra.*

The only type of disposition that can produce the problem that the regulations address is a pecuniary disposition that (i) is satisfiable in kind at other than date-of-distribution values or (ii) is satisfiable without compensation (or with compensation that is too small or too large) for lapse of time between the date of death and the date of satisfaction or (iii) is satisfiable as described in both (i) and (ii). Fortunately, from the perspective of facility of administration, the fiduciary can avoid complying with the complicated rules concerning delayed payment by satisfying or setting aside the pecuniary disposition within 15 months after the death of the transferor.

If the Code requires the denominator of the applicable fraction to include values at dates of distribution but the governing instrument provides for the funding of the pecuniary disposition on the basis of other values, the applicable fraction can have a denominator that is not determinable when the estate tax return is due and the transferor's executor must allocate the GST exemption and thus fix the numerator. Uncertainty about the size of the denominator can generate uncertainty about the desired size of the numerator and about the amount of GST exemption that is available for allocation among various dispositions. While allocation of GST exemption by means of a formula can produce the desired inclusion ratio, it cannot dissipate the uncertainty.

The planning implication is to use in the governing instrument a system of funding that requires valuation that coincides with what the Code requires. Two systems of funding, each used separately, seem to permit this result:

1. Require allocation of assets in kind at values at dates of distribution (that is, use a "true" pecuniary formula) and fund according to the mandate; or
2. Require allocation of assets in kind at estate tax values (that is, use a fractional share formula, and, optionally, permit the fiduciary to deviate from strict fractionalization by substituting assets among shares on the basis of values at the time of allocation, or use a "64-19" formula that describes a pecuniary amount but provides for its satisfaction in kind at estate tax values with ratable sharing of

appreciation and depreciation of all assets that are available for allocation) and fund according to the mandate.

§ 7.02(b) Effect upon Planning for Marital Deduction

If the predeceasing spouse wants to use his or her previously unallocated GST exemption but avoid the payment of estate tax upon his or her death, his or her executor might have to allocate his or her exemption upon his or her death to a disposition that qualifies for the marital deduction.

§ 7.02(b)(1) Qualified Terminable Interest Property ("QTIP") Is Necessary

Property that only is included in the gross estate of the surviving spouse because of a QTIP election is the only form of disposition that both allows full use of the GST exemption of the predeceasing spouse and does not generate transfer tax until the death of the surviving spouse. The executor of the predeceasing spouse can elect, according to Code Section 2652(a)(3), to treat a QTIP election as though it is not made and thus effectively can elect that the predeceasing spouse be the transferor for generation-skipping tax purposes.

The statute, as originally enacted, might have permitted the executor to limit the Code Section 2652(a)(3) election to such specific portion (that is, fraction or percentage) of the QTIP as was necessary fully to absorb the GST exemption of the predeceasing spouse. However, the statute as amended requires that the election be with respect to all of the property in a particular trust. Since the election inherently affects only QTIP, effectively the statute requires that the election be with respect to all of the QTIP in the particular trust. If a Code Section 2652(a)(3) election is desirable for less than all of the QTIP, the rule requires a two-step procedure, in a particular sequence.

1. First, by means of a mandate in the governing instrument or a fiduciary's exercise of discretion, create two trusts. The rules that apply generally to the discretionary sever-

ance of a trust apply also to the discretionary severance of a QTIP trust.[14]

2. Second, make the Code Section 2652(a)(3) election for all of the property in one of the trusts.

§ 7.02(b)(2) Amount of QTIP That Is Required

If the predeceasing spouse wants to avoid payment of estate tax upon his or her death but yet use all of his or her unallocated GST exemption, QTIP is necessary only to such extent as the GST exemption unallocated during life exceeds the value (for purposes of determining the inclusion ratio) of the property in the credit shelter disposition that, unless exempt, might produce a generation-skipping transfer. The foregoing principles indicate that perhaps the executor of the predeceasing spouse should allocate the GST exemption to QTIP only to the extent the exemption is not properly allocable to a credit shelter disposition. Further, spouses who might be willing to accept the relative rigidity of QTIP only to such extent as is necessary to allow full use of their GST exemptions might wish to use other than QTIP for the balance of the marital disposition.

§ 7.02(b)(3) Use of Disclaimer To Create QTIP

If a governing instrument otherwise would not permit the full use of the GST exemption of a predeceasing spouse without generating liability for estate tax before the death of the surviving spouse, the surviving spouse yet might permit deferral of the tax by using a disclaimer to create a disposition with respect to which the executor of the predeceasing spouse can make QTIP and Code Section 2652(a)(3) elections and allocate the GST exemption of the predeceasing spouse. A surviving spouse's disclaimer for the purpose of creating qualified terminable interest property contemplates a disclaimer of a disposition that, but for the disclaimer, would be included in the completed gifts or gross estate of the surviving spouse. Unlike the usual subject of a qualified disclaimer, the principal purpose of this disclaimer is to create a disposition with different tax attributes but not to create a disposition

---

[14]See § 7.02(a)(2)(B), *supra*.

that is excluded from the completed gifts or gross estate of the disclaimant.

Does attainment of this unusual purpose require a disclaimer that is "qualified?" Assume that the original disposition is an outright gift or a trust from which the spouse can withdraw all principal at will. A disclaimer that is not qualified and causes the spouse to have neither ownership of, nor a general power to appoint, the principal has the effect of transferring the remainder interest in a transfer for gift tax or estate tax purposes.

Whether or not the nonqualified disclaimer produces a gift that immediately is taxable, the critical question is whether the occurrence of a transfer for gift tax purposes or estate tax purposes prevents recognition of the disclaimer for generation-skipping tax purposes. A nonqualified disclaimer seems to cause the disclaimant to be regarded, for generation-skipping tax purposes, as having received and transferred the disclaimed interests. If the surviving spouse is deemed to receive the principal, the deemed receipt includes the principal in the completed gifts or gross estate of the surviving spouse *other than because the property is QTIP.* Thus, it causes the surviving spouse to be the transferor for generation-skipping tax purposes *regardless* of whether the executor of the predeceasing spouse makes a Code Section 2652(a)(3) election.

Based on the foregoing, use of a disclaimer to create qualified terminable interest property for which a predeceased spouse can be the "transferor" for generation-skipping tax purposes requires a qualified disclaimer. Therefore, it requires either (i) a disposition that conforms to the QTIP criteria after the disclaimant disclaims each "separate interest" that fails to conform, or (ii) a receptacle that (originally or because of a disclaimer of each "'separate interest" that fails to conform) conforms to the QTIP criteria.[15] Additionally, in each case, it requires that the spouse not have any power to direct beneficial enjoyment.[16]

§ 7.02(b)(4) Division into Portions

The precepts about the use of separate funds for different

---

[15]*See* Treas. Reg. § 25.2518-3(a)(1)(i), and Code § 2518(b)(4)(A).

[16]Code § 2518(b)(4).

transferors and for exempt and nonexempt property and about the Code Section 2652(a)(3) election can suggest the division and the ordered use, during the life or upon the death of the donee or surviving spouse, of property that can qualify as QTIP into five portions and two subportions.

§ 7.02(b)(4)(A) Portion Number One. Portion Number One qualifies for the marital deduction and is exempt for generation-skipping tax purposes. The donor or predeceased spouse remains as its transferor after it is included in the completed gifts or gross estate of the other spouse.[17]

QTIP and Code Section 2652(a)(3) elections are made. The donor or predeceased spouse's GST exemption is allocated.

§ 7.02(b)(4)(B) Portion Number Two. Portion Number Two qualifies for the marital deduction and is not exempt for generation-skipping tax purposes. The donor or predeceased spouse remains as its transferor after it is included in the completed gifts or gross estate of the other spouse.

QTIP and Code Section 2652(a)(3) elections are made. No GST exemption is allocated. Although an election is possible under Code Section 2652(a)(3) to treat the donor or predeceasing spouse as the transferor of QTIP to which the GST exemption of the donor or predeceasing spouse is not allocated, generally (but not always) an allocation of the GST exemption should coincide with the election. Generally, the only purpose for the election is to permit the use of the GST exemption of the donor (or predeceasing) spouse notwithstanding that the exempt property is to be included in the completed gifts or gross estate of the other spouse. If no GST exemption of the donor or predeceasing spouse is to be allocated, a failure to elect promotes flexibility by permitting allocation of the GST exemption of the other spouse and upon the death of the other spouse avoids transforming into a taxable termination what otherwise would be a direct skip to which the predeceased child exception might apply. However, treatment of the donor or predeceasing spouse as the transferor of nonexempt property (that is, property to which an election is made under Code Section 2652(a)(3) but to which no GST exemption of the

[17] See Appendix, Form #2, *infra*.

donor or predeceasing spouse is allocated) might make sense if a holder of the succeeding interest is a non-skip person with respect to the grantor but is a skip person with respect to the grantor's spouse.

§ 7.02(b)(4)(C) Portion Number Three. Portion Number Three qualifies for the marital deduction and is not exempt for generation-skipping tax purposes during the life of the donee or surviving spouse. The donee or surviving spouse becomes its transferor when the property is included in his or her completed gifts or gross estate.[18]

A QTIP election is made, but no Code Section 2652(a)(3) election is made. Therefore, no GST exemption of the donor or predeceased spouse is allocated. The anticipated allocation of the GST exemption of the donee or surviving spouse to property in this portion may suggest a further division before the allocation, into a subportion that will be wholly exempt and a subportion that will be wholly nonexempt.[19]

§ 7.02(b)(4)(D) Portion Number Four. Portion Number Four does not qualify for the marital deduction and is exempt for generation-skipping tax purposes. The donor or predeceased spouse remains as its transferor after the death of the other spouse.

No QTIP election is made. Therefore, no Code Section 2652(a)(3) election is made. The donor or predeceased spouse's GST exemption is allocated.

§ 7.02(b)(4)(E) Portion Number Five. Portion Number Five does not qualify for the marital deduction and is not exempt for generation-skipping tax purposes. The donor or predeceased spouse remains as its transferor after the death of the other spouse.

No QTIP election is made. Therefore, no Code Section 2652(a)(3) election is made. No GST exemption is allocated.

§ 7.02(b)(4)(F) The Order of Distributions and of Paying Taxes from the Portions. Generally, the fiduciary should make distributions to the donee or surviving spouse, and (in the case of the marital portions) pay death taxes upon the death of the donee or surviving spouse, from the portions in the following order, subject, however,

---

[18] *Id.*

[19] See Appendix, Form #1, *infra.*

to reversing the first and second categories if the transferee upon the death of the donee or surviving spouse is a non-skip person relative to the donor or predeceased spouse but is a skip person relative to the donee or surviving spouse:

1. Marital, nonexempt, donor or predeceased spouse is transferor (that is, Portion Number Two);
2. Marital, nonexempt, donee or surviving spouse is transferor (that is, Portion Number Three);
3. Marital, exempt (that is, Portion Number One);
4. Nonmarital, nonexempt (that is, Portion Number Five); and
5. Nonmarital, exempt (that is, Portion Number Four).

§ 7.02(c) Effect upon Ownership of Property

Spouses should consider structuring their transfers and the ownership of their property to enable them fully to use *each* of their GST exemptions regardless of who dies first.

If the wealthier spouse dies first and structures his or her transfers properly, no *inter vivos,* interspousal transfer is necessary to avoid wasting any GST exemption of either spouse. The GST exemption of the wealthier spouse is usable upon his or her death. The surviving spouse can allocate his or her own GST exemption to any property that is included in his or her gross estate but that is not QTIP with respect to which the predeceasing spouse is the transferor because of an election according to Code Section 2652(a)(3).

If the spouses wish to preserve the ability fully to use two GST exemptions even if the less wealthy spouse dies first, two procedures are available.

First, splitting of gifts according to Code Section 2513(a) permits a less wealthy spouse fully to use a GST exemption even though the exemption exceeds the property of the less wealthy spouse. This procedure requires a transfer of property to a third party before the death of the predeceasing spouse. Some spouses will not want to transfer property to a third party until the death of the surviving, or, at least, the predeceasing, spouse.

Second, the spouses can hedge against the prior death of the less wealthy spouse, and the consequent loss of his or her GST exemption, by rearranging ownership of their property and by the wealthier spouse making a gift to the less wealthy spouse. The general principle is that the amount which the wealthier spouse must transfer is the amount of property of the wealthier spouse which (after deducting debts, funeral expenses, costs of administration, and death taxes) both (i) exceeds his or her unused GST exemption, and (ii) if added to the property of the less wealthy spouse, would not cause the property of the less wealthy spouse (after deducting debts, funeral expenses, costs of administration, and death taxes) to exceed the unused GST exemption of the less wealthy spouse.

Subprinciples are helpful to apply the general principle. If (assuming each spouse died immediately) the combined transfers that would be taxable for estate tax purposes, minus the aggregate death taxes, would be less than one GST exemption (that is, $1,000,000), either spouse can own as much of the property as he or she wishes, since no transfer is necessary fully to exempt all of the property. If (assuming each spouse died immediately) the combined transfers that would be taxable for estate tax purposes, minus the aggregate death taxes, would be between one and two times the GST exemption (that is, between $1,000,000 and $2,000,000), the wealthier spouse should have what (assuming each spouse died immediately) would be a gross estate (net of debts, funeral expenses, costs of administration, and death taxes) not exceeding his or her unused GST exemption, and the less wealthy spouse should have the balance. If (assuming each spouse died immediately) the combined transfers that would be taxable for estate tax purposes, minus the aggregate death taxes, would be larger than two times the GST exemption (that is, $2,000,000), the less wealthy spouse should have what (assuming each spouse died immediately) would be a gross estate (net of debts, funeral expenses, costs of administration, and death taxes) equal to his or her unused GST exemption, and the wealthier spouse should have the balance. A *sine qua non* to the success of an interspousal, lifetime giving program which is designed to permit full use of two GST exemptions but not generate estate tax until the death of the surviving spouse is that, to the extent of his or her unused GST exemption, a predeceasing, donee spouse must cause himself or herself to be the "transferor" by leaving his or her property either in such a manner as will by-pass the completed gifts and gross estate of the surviving, donor spouse, or in QTIP.

§ 7.02(d) Effect upon Various Types of Transfers Including Those That Automatically Are Exempt Without Allocation of GST Exemption.

The general theory of allocation of GST exemption is also usable to compare the relative efficiencies of various types of transfers including nontaxable, lifetime gifts that automatically are exempt from the generation-skipping tax without any allocation of GST exemption. The principal advantage of those gifts is that they do not consume GST exemption. Their principal disadvantages are that they skip only one generation and they require a format that permits the donee to control the disposition at death, and perhaps also during life.

Comparison of Various Lifetime Gifts

1. Nontaxable gift, outright.
   a. No gift tax cost.
   b. "Avoids" only one generation-skipping transfer.
   c. Generation-skipping tax is avoided presently.
   d. The donee must have control.
   e. Does not require use of GST exemption.
2. Nontaxable gift to a Code Section 2642(c) trust for a skip person.
   a. No gift tax cost.
   b. "Avoids" only one generation-skipping transfer.
   c. Generation-skipping tax is avoided presently.
   d. The donee must have control.
   e. Does not require use of GST exemption.
3. Nontaxable gift to a trust (non-Code Section 2642(c)) for a non skip person.
   a. No gift tax cost.
   b. Can "avoid" multiple generation-skipping transfers.

   c. Generation-skipping tax is avoided only in the future.
   d. Does not require the donee to have control.
   e. Requires use of GST exemption.
4. Unified credit gift.
   a. Generates opportunity cost.
   b. Can "avoid" multiple generation-skipping transfers.
   c. Generation-skipping tax is avoided presently or in the future, or both presently and in the future.
   d. Does not require the donee to have control.
   e. Requires use of GST exemption.
5. Taxable gift.
   a. Requires payment of gift tax.
   b. Can "avoid" multiple generation-skipping transfers.
   c. Generation-skipping tax is avoided presently or in the future, or both presently and in the future.
   d. Does not require the donee to have control.
   e. Requires use of GST exemption.

Comparison of Deathtime Transfers and Lifetime Gifts

1. Deathtime transfers in excess of the amount that the unified credit can shelter require payment of estate tax.
2. Deathtime transfers can "avoid" multiple generation-skipping transfers.
3. Deathtime transfers can avoid generation-skipping tax presently or in the future, or both presently and in the future.
4. Deathtime transfers do not require the donee to have control.
5. Deathtime transfers require use of GST exemption. If death has occurred, the question of when to incur gift tax or estate tax does not exist, and the only monetary issue is to determine which disposition to exempt.

§ 7.03 USING ANNUAL EXCLUSION GIFTS TO SKIP GENERATIONS

§ 7.03(a) In General

Any transfer of property to the extent the transfer is excluded from the donor's taxable gifts by reason of an annual exclusion according to Code Section 2503(b), after application of gift-splitting according to Code Section 2513(a), is a "nontaxable gift." Certain nontaxable gifts are exempt from the generation-skipping tax.

A transferor directly can skip one or more generations by means of a direct skip that is a nontaxable gift outside any trust. This type of a transfer benefits only one person before it loses its exemption from transfer tax.

Before April 1, 1988, a donor could use an annual exclusion gift to benefit more than one person, including in more than one generation, exempt from generation-skipping tax. The donor used for this purpose a nontaxable gift to an individual by means of an interest in a trust.

If this type of gift were to have skipped one or more generations at the level of the donee or lower than the level of the donee, the gift must have escaped inclusion in the completed gifts and gross estate of the donee. Although a gift of an income interest to an individual can be an annual exclusion gift within Code Section 2503(b), it effectively includes the income interest (but not the underlying property) in the completed gifts or gross estate of the donee and, therefore, does not skip the generation to which the donee is assigned or any lower generation.

The more promising example was a contribution to a trust with an individual granted an interest by means of an absolute right to withdraw the property, that is, a *Crummey* power.[20] To such extent as the lapse of a right to withdraw is within the limitations of the "five-and-five" exception[21] to the definition of a general power of appointment, the lapse is not a transfer for gift tax or

---

[20] *See* Crummey v. Commissioner, 397 F.2d 82 (9th Cir. 1968). See also § 6.09(b), *supra,* and § 7.03(b)(3), *infra.*

[21] Five percent or $5,000.

estate tax purposes.[22] Therefore, the lapse avoids inclusion of the subject property in the completed taxable gifts and gross estate of the donee. Moreover, it does not create a new transferor or dissipate any exemption of the property from the generation-skipping tax.

Conversely, to such extent as the lapse of a right to withdraw exceeds the limitations of the "five-and-five" exception to the definition of a general power of appointment, the lapse is a transfer for gift tax or estate tax purposes. A lapse that is not within the "five-and-five" exception causes the donee to become the transferor and dissipates any exemption for the original transferor's gift. Before April, 1988, whether the property remained outside the orbit of the generation-skipping tax after the lapse depended upon whether the resulting gift, itself, was a "nontaxable gift." Even if the donee's resulting gift is a completed gift, it lowers the transferor to the generation of the original donee and lowers the generation at which any individual is a skip person.

§ 7.03(b) Transfers and Exemptions After March 1988

§ 7.03(b)(1) In General

Effective with respect to transfers after March 31, 1988, no annual exclusion gift is exempt from the generation-skipping tax unless the gift benefits only one person before it again becomes subject to gift tax or estate tax. Consistently, any annual exclusion gift that is to an individual and is not to a trust is exempt from the generation-skipping tax. However, again consistently, any annual exclusion gift "to a trust" is exempt from the generation-skipping tax only if

1. The trust property is not distributable to any person other than the donee during the life of the donee, and
2. The trust property is includable in the gross estate of the donee for estate tax purposes if the trust does not terminate before the donee dies.[23]

---

[22] Code §§ 2041(b)(2) and 2514(e).

[23] Code § 2642(c).

§ 7.03(b)(2) *Present-Interest Trust for a Minor*

A present-interest trust for a minor, described in Code Section 2503(c), meets this description.

§ 7.03(b)(3) *Certain* Crummey *Trusts*

A trust also meets these criteria if (i) the donee is the only permissible distributee during the donee's life, (ii) the donee has a *Crummey* power with respect to each gift so that each gift is a present interest which is excludable for gift tax purposes, and (iii) the donee has a general power to appoint by will so that the trust property is included in the gross estate of the donee.

§ 7.03(b)(4) *A Gift "to a Trust"*

The entire amount of any gift which is subject to a *Crummey* power is a gift "to a trust," notwithstanding that for gift tax purposes the gift is regarded as a gift to an individual.[24]

§ 7.03(b)(5) *Trusts That Do Not Meet Requirements for GST Purposes*

Preservation of an inclusion ratio of zero for any transfer after March 31, 1988, including any gift that is subject to a *Crummey* power, to a trust that does not meet the criteria that are required to exempt the gift for generation-skipping tax purposes requires allocation of GST exemption of the transferor. For example, if GST exemption is not allocated, all direct skips to a trust absorb an automatic allocation of GST exemption or, to any extent that unallocated GST exemption is insufficient or the transferor elects to avoid the automatic allocation, immediately create liability for generation-skipping tax. However, if a non-skip person has an interest in the trust, the trust is not a skip person, and a transfer that for gift tax purposes is regarded (because of a *Crummey* power) as a transfer to an individual below the level of child is a transfer that for generation-skipping tax purposes is not a direct skip. Similarly, again if GST exemption is not allocated, all other gifts (for example, to a child) that for generation-skipping tax purposes are regarded as transfers to a trust produce an inclusion ratio of more

---

[24]Prop. Treas. Reg. § 26.2652-1(a)(5), Ex. 5, 57 Fed. Reg. 31368 (1992).

than zero. If the original gift is not a direct skip and a subsequent exercise or lapse of the donee's right to withdraw causes the donee to become the transferor, the subsequent exercise or lapse wastes, to that extent, any previous allocation of the GST exemption of the donor.

§ 7.04 USING "QUALIFIED TRANSFERS" TO SKIP GENERATIONS

Any transfer that, if made by a person during life, would be a "qualified transfer" according to Code Section 2503(e) is a non-taxable gift that is exempt from the generation-skipping tax.[25]

§ 7.04(a) Types of Qualified Transfers

Qualified transfers include payments made on behalf of a person directly (i) to an educational institution for tuition for the person or (ii) to a provider of medical care for the person. Except for the exemption, a trustee's distribution of trust property on behalf of a skip person for either of these purposes would be a taxable distribution. The draftsperson should consider enhancing the ability and the inclination of trustees and of donees of nongeneral powers of appointment to make these transfers.

Since a payment that discharges the legal obligation of a person to provide for the education or medical care of another may be a payment to the obligor (and thus not a qualified transfer within Code Section 2503(e)), perhaps the trustee should make (and the donee of the power to appoint be permitted to make) only payments that do not discharge any legal obligation that one person owes to another. A trustee's unexercised (or, perhaps, even exercised) discretionary ability to use trust property to satisfy the legal obligation of a person to support another person is ignored *for purposes of determining whether the obligor has an "interest."*[26] However, it is doubtful that this rule affects whether a transfer is a qualified transfer according to Code Section 2503(e).

---

[25] Code § 2611(b)(1); *see also* Code § 2642(c)(3).

[26] Code § 2652(c).

§ 7.05 FACILITATING GRANDCHILD EXCLUSIONS

§ 7.05(a) Background

When, before 1990, the grandchild exclusion was available, the potential exclusion was $8,000,000 for each grandchild, being $4,000,000 for transfers from each set of grandparents. Two million dollars of transfers before 1990 were excludable from direct skips to each grandchild of the transferor. Each grandchild had four grandparents, and each grandparent was a potential transferor.

Each set of grandparents that wished to maximize the use of grandchild exclusions should have held and disposed of its property in such a manner as would have permitted each spouse to have been the transferor of $2,000,000 per grandchild in a transfer that, except for the exclusion, would have been a direct skip. A grandparent could have transferred his or her own property or property that was included in his or her gross estate in a non-QTIP marital deduction trust. Alternatively, a grandparent (or his or her executor) could have failed to elect to disregard a QTIP election for generation-skipping tax purposes and thus could have allowed his or her spouse to have been the "transferor" of the QTIP that was included in the completed gifts or gross estate of the donee or surviving grandparent. Alternatively, a grandparent could have allowed his or her spouse to have been deemed to have been the transferor of a lifetime gift that was split according to Code Section 2513(a).[27]

§ 7.05(b) Qualifying for the Grandchild Exclusion from Direct Skips

If a transfer in trust was to have passed "to" a grandchild of the transferor and thus was to have qualified for the grandchild exclusion from direct skips, the dispositive instrument must not have permitted diversion of the property from the grandchild to any other person during the grandchild's life. *If* a trustee (or a custodian of a gift under the Uniform Gifts to Minors Act or Uniform Transfers to Minors Act) ("UGMA" or "UTMA") could have distributed property with the effect of discharging a legal obliga-

---

[27]Code § 2652(a)(2).

tion (for example, an obligation of support) of someone other than the grandchild, the trustee arguably possessed the proscribed power.[28] A trustee's unexercised (or, perhaps, even exercised), discretionary ability to use trust property to satisfy the legal obligation of a person to support another person is ignored *for purposes of determining whether the obligor has an "interest."* However, it is unclear whether this ability is similarly ignored for purposes of determining whether a transfer was "to" a grandchild.

This writer reiterates that a payment which discharges a legal obligation owed by a person to the nominal distributee (that is, the grandchild) arguably is a distribution to the obligor and not to the obligee and, therefore, the fiduciary arguably does not have any power to make it.[29] If, nevertheless, the problem could have existed, the draftsperson might have avoided it in a trust (but not in an UGMA or UTMA arrangement) by including a provision such as the following:

> The Trustee shall not make (or have any power to make) any payment that would discharge any legal obligation of any person to whom the trustee cannot make payment directly.

Similarly, if a trustee could have paid property (perhaps pursuant to a facility-of-payment clause) to someone who had either no defined fiduciary duty or a poorly defined fiduciary duty (for example, a guardian or conservator of the person, as opposed to a guardian or conservator of the estate, of the beneficiary), an issue might have existed concerning diversion of the property from the grandchild. The cautious draftsperson might have addressed this issue by permitting the fiduciary to make payment only (i) to entities that had statutorily and/or judicially-defined fiduciary obligations to use the property in particular ways for the grandchild, (ii) in reimbursement of funds properly advanced by the recipient for the grandchild, or (iii) to the grandchild himself or herself.

Consider, for example, the following language:

---

[28] *Cf.* Upjohn v. United States, 72-2 USTC ¶ 12,888 (W.D. Mich. 1972).

[29] See § 6.09, *supra.*

> *Distributions to Certain Persons.* Property becoming payable to, or for the benefit of, a person who is under a minority or other legal disability or who is unable properly to manage it shall be paid in the discretion of the Trustee (i) directly to the person or (ii) to the guardian or conservator of the person's estate or (iii) to any custodian for the person under any applicable Uniform Gifts or Transfers to Minors Act or (iv) directly for the benefit of the person (including in reimbursement for amounts properly advanced for the person's benefit).

§ 7.05(c) Qualifying for the Grandchild Exclusion Because of a Child's Disclaimer

Property that passed to a grandchild because of a child's disclaimer could have qualified for the grandchild exclusion. A governing instrument could have contemplated this type of disclaimer and enhanced flexibility by permitting the child to determine whether to accept or disclaim the subject property, in whole or in part.

§ 7.05(d) The Draftsman's Considerations for Vesting a Transfer

If property could have passed to a trust for a grandchild because a child either disclaimed the transfer or predeceased the grandchild, the draftsperson would not have known in advance how, if at all, property would have reached the trust. Therefore, the draftsperson might have used for the grandchild a trust that could have received both transfers that were to qualify for the grandchild exclusion from direct skips and other transfers. The governing instrument might have vested a transfer in the grandchild for estate tax purposes only to such extent as the vesting caused the transfer not to be a generation-skipping transfer. The governing instrument might have vested any transfer that, even if not vested, would not have been a direct skip because the transfer was within the predeceased child exception or that, even if vested, would have been a direct skip because the transfer was after 1989 or exceeded the dollar limitation.

§ 7.06 MAXIMIZING PREDECEASED CHILD EXCEPTIONS

Typically, the dispositions of each of two spouses for their descendants upon the death of the surviving spouse are the same regardless of which of the spouses is the survivor. Accordingly, if the spouse of the testator survives both the testator and a child of the testator (or of the spouse of the testator) and the instrument creates a share for the children of the deceased child, whether property of which one spouse is the transferor rather than property of which the other is the transferor satisfies the disposition often is a matter of indifference for nontax purposes. However, for tax purposes, the passage to this share of property of which the testator is the transferor is a taxable termination, but the passage to this share of property of which the spouse of the testator is the transferor qualifies for the predeceased child exception and is not a generation-skipping transfer. Accordingly, allocation to this disposition of property of which the spouse of the testator, rather than the testator, is the transferor — that is, substitution of property of one person for property of another, can avoid a generation-skipping transfer. If the share for the child of the deceased child is to pass outright, this substitution need not alter beneficial enjoyment or distort the dispositive arrangement. However, if the share for the child of the predeceased child is to pass in such a manner as to avoid inclusion in the gross estate of the grandchild, qualification of the share for the predeceased child exception will cause a generation-skipping tax when the share passes to descendants of the grandchild upon the death of the grandchild and will cause the descendants of the grandchild to receive less than if GST exemption were allocated to the share.

Even after the death of a predeceasing spouse, the surviving spouse might make the substitution and thus maximize the predeceased child exception. A first procedure requires the surviving spouse to have a nongeneral power to alter, at least among the descendants of the predeceased spouse, the disposition that the predeceased spouse created. The surviving spouse can exercise the power by directing property of which the predeceased spouse is the transferor in favor of surviving children. The surviving spouse can make a compensating distribution of property of which the surviving spouse is the transferor in favor of children of a predeceased child.

Alternatively, the draftsperson seems able to accomplish the substitution by causing the governing instrument to require it.[30]

A third procedure, of uncertain effect, is the exercise of authority to make non-pro rata distributions for the purpose of changing the identity of the transferor.[31]

§ 7.07 LINKING SOURCES AND USES OF PROPERTY TO OPTIMIZE USE OF GST EXEMPTIONS, ANNUAL EXCLUSION GIFTS, QUALIFIED TRANSFERS, AND PREDECEASED CHILD EXCEPTIONS

§ 7.07(a) The Various Preferences Accord Favorable Treatment

The various preferences accord favorable treatment to (i) particular property (that is, property that has an inclusion ratio of zero or a particular transferor) and (ii) particular dispositions (that is, dispositions that qualify for the predeceased child exception or that are transfers to non-skip persons or that are exempt, excluded gifts).

§ 7.07(a)(1) Efficient Use of Favored Property

Efficient use of favored property is a function of (i) creation and preservation of certain types of property, separately from other property, and (ii) allocation of particular property to particular dispositions (that is, allocation of property that is favored with an inclusion ratio of zero to dispositions that are not favored).

§ 7.07(a)(2) Efficient Use of Favored Dispositions

Efficient use of favored dispositions is a function of (i) compliance with the tax prerequisites for the dispositions, and (ii) allocation of particular property to them (that is, property that is not favored with a low inclusion ratio).

---

[30] See Appendix, Form #6, *infra*.

[31] See § 7.07(a)(4), *infra*.

§ 7.07(a)(3) Creation and Preservation of Favored and Not Favored Property

Creation and preservation of different categories of property requires segregation of property by reference to tax attributes.[32] The segregation must exist even during the time that the interim disposition of property with different attributes is not different. The segregation often must continue until the property is expended or is ultimately distributed outright.

§ 7.07(a)(4) Efficient Linkage of Particular Disposition and Particular Property

Efficient linkage of a particular disposition, on the one hand, and the property that has the most appropriate attributes to satisfy it, on the other, suggests the usefulness of non-pro rata allocation of various funds of property to various dispositions.[33] This type of non-pro rata allocation is not the familiar type that permits a fiduciary to allocate various properties in a single fund non-pro rata to various dispositions but requires pro rata allocation of the value of each fund among the various dispositions.

This type of non-pro rata allocation need not distort the dispositive arrangement viewed in the aggregate. First, the testator can construct certain dispositions that exist, by their terms, only to any extent that favored — that is, exempt — property is available to satisfy them or that the dispositions are favored — that is, exempt — gifts. Second, the governing instrument generally can permit non-pro rata allocations only to such extent as dispositions, viewed in the aggregate, are not altered.

As to each of the following illustrations, consider whether the non-pro rata allocation, pursuant to the fiduciary's exercise of discretion, will govern for generation-skipping tax purposes. Would the non-pro rata allocation have a better chance of prevailing if it were pursuant to a mandate rather than pursuant to discretion? Although a mandate appears feasible, it might inject an undesirable degree of rigidity and produce improper results in some situations.

---

[32]See Appendix, Form #1, *infra*.

[33]See Appendix, Form #5, *infra*.

Illustration 1:

Assume that a person creates by will a $2,000,000 trust for the benefit of his or her two children until the younger attains 21 years of age, at which time the trust is to be distributed to the descendants of the grantor then living, per stirpes. All $1,000,000 of the GST exemption of the grantor is available for allocation to property in this trust. A child dies one year after the death of the grantor and leaves a descendant surviving. Two years after the death of the grantor, the other child of the grantor attains 21 years of age.

Since the grantor's executor must allocate GST exemption no later than the due date for the grantor's estate tax return (which is before the trust is split into shares), the executor cannot allocate GST exemption to the share that will pass to the descendant of the deceased child. Therefore, the grantor's executor must allocate the exemption to the entire trust, or if the governing instrument permits, the fiduciary can split the trust into two and the grantor's executor can allocate the exemption to cause one of the two to be exempt. Based upon the principles previously discussed, the fiduciary and the executor select the latter alternative.

Assuming no change in value, pro rata allocation of each fund would require the distribution of $500,000 from each to the descendant of the deceased child (thus producing a taxable transfer of $500,000) and the distribution of $500,000 from each to the living child (thus wasting the exemption for $500,000 of property). Again assuming no change in value, the described non-pro rata allocation, on the other hand, would involve the distribution of all of the exempt fund to the descendant of the deceased child and the distribution of all of the nonexempt fund to the living child and, thus, would not produce any taxable transfer or waste any GST exemption.

This *Illustration 1* depicts one transferor and an attempt to alter the proportions of his or her exempt property and his or her nonexempt property, respectively, that are distributed to particular individuals.

Illustration 2:

Assume that upon the death of the survivor of two spouses, a $1,000,000 exempt fund of which the predeceasing spouse is the transferor (perhaps a nonmarital trust to which the executor of the predeceasing spouse allocated all of the GST exemption of the predeceasing spouse) and a $1,000,000 nonexempt fund of which the surviving spouse is the transferor (perhaps QTIP to which none of the GST exemption of the surviving spouse is allocated) are to be distributed one half to a skip person and one half to a non-skip person.

Pro rata allocation of each fund would require the distribution of $500,000 from each to the skip person (thus producing a taxable transfer of $500,000) and the distribution of $500,000 from each to the non-skip person (thus wasting the exemption for $500,000 of property). The described non-pro rata allocation, on the other hand, would involve the distribution of all of the exempt fund to the skip person and the distribution of all of the nonexempt fund to the non-skip person and thus might not produce any taxable transfer or waste any GST exemption.

Although the predeceased spouse is the transferor of the exempt fund and the surviving spouse is the transferor of the nonexempt fund, the identity of the transferor (in contrast to *Illustration 3*), does not control whether a generation-skipping transfer will, or will not, occur.

This *Illustration 2* depicts an attempt to alter the proportions of the exempt property and the nonexempt property, respectively, that are distributed to particular individuals. The purpose of the non-pro rata allocation is the same as in *Illustration 1, supra.* However, unlike *Illustration 1, Illustration 2* involves two transferors.

> ***Illustration 3:***
>
> **Assume the same facts as in *Illustration 2,* except that the person designated as a skip person is a skip person only with respect to transfers of which the predeceased spouse is the transferor and is a non-skip person with respect to transfers of which the surviving spouse is the transferor. This phenomenon can occur either because of the age of the designated person relative to the age of the transferor or because the designated person is a child of a predeceased child of the transferor (or of the transferor's spouse or former spouse).**

Unlike *Illustration 2,* in *Illustration 3* the identity of the transferor *does* control whether a generation-skipping transfer will, or will not, occur. *Illustration 3* depicts the use of non-pro rata distributions for the purpose of avoiding a generation-skipping transfer by altering the identity of the transferor of the property that a particular distributee will receive.

The draftsperson should appreciate the possibility that the exercise of this authority to make non-pro rata distributions is ineffective to characterize particular transfers as consisting of exempt or nonexempt property. A greater possibility of ineffectiveness might exist when the purpose or the effect is to allocate property transferred by one transferor rather than property transferred by another. The greatest possibility of ineffectiveness might exist when the purpose of using the non-pro rata authority is to change the identity of the transferor in order to cause a particular distributee to be a non-skip person rather than a skip person.

§ 7.07(a)(5) Drafting Techniques Appropriate for Linkages of Property and Dispositions

Drafting techniques appear available to permit or require the appropriate linkage of property and dispositions. Upon the death of the surviving spouse, some draftspersons collect in one receptacle all exempt property from various funds and collect in another receptacle all nonexempt property from various funds, and they dispose of each receptacle in a parallel manner or separately. While this system takes into account whether the property is exempt, it fails to take into account the identity of the transferor. If the instrument includes any disposition to a person who, because of relative ages or the predeceased child exception, is a skip person if one spouse is the transferor but is a non-skip person if the other spouse is the transferor and, therefore, the disposition is a generation-skipping transfer if one spouse is the transferor but is not a generation-skipping transfer if the other spouse is the transferor, satisfaction of the disposition with exempt property might waste GST exemption, and satisfaction of it with nonexempt property might create unnecessary liability for tax. Even if the portions of a trust that are attributable to different transferors are treated as separate trusts, pro rata use of each presents the described problem.

Upon the death of the surviving spouse, other draftspersons collect in one receptacle all exempt property from various funds, collect in another receptacle all nonexempt property (from various funds) of which the survivor is the transferor, and collect in a third receptacle all nonexempt property (from various funds) of which the predeceased spouse is the transferor, and they dispose of each receptacle in a parallel manner or separately.

Unless authorization to make the described type of non-pro rata distributions is sufficient to avoid the problem, a governing instrument that contains a disposition to a skip person and a disposition to a non-skip person and that disposes of each receptacle in a parallel manner might produce the same result as if property never were segregated by reference to attributes.

For example, assume that the ultimate disposition is one half to a child and one half to the child's child. Pro rata allocation of the value of each fund of property might fail to optimize allocation of either nonexempt or exempt property. Similarly, assume that the ultimate disposition is one half to a trust for a child (remainder to a grandchild) and one half to a child of a predeceased child. Pro rata allocation of the value of each fund of property might fail to optimize allocation of nonexempt property of which the surviving spouse is the transferor and, correspondingly, might fail to optimize allocation of exempt property and of nonexempt property of which the predeceasing spouse is the transferor.

If, on the other hand, the governing instrument requires the use of particular, segregated funds in a specified order (rather than pro rata) to satisfy particular dispositions (which exist regardless of the character of the property available to satisfy them), or if, alternatively, the instrument causes the character of dispositions to vary depending upon the character of the property available to satisfy them, the system might produce a proper result. However, the system requires custom drafting that, given the complexity of the objectives and the number of combinations and permutations, is difficult and time-consuming.

Alternatively, the draftsperson can consider a system that does not require combinations of funds, based upon that which is exempt or nonexempt, upon the death of the surviving spouse. The alternative system permits segregation of property with different tax attributes and authorizes the described type of non-pro rata allocation of funds subject to the constraint that the allocation not alter dispositions considered in the aggregate.[34] However, the alternative system is not appropriate to use if ultimate dispositions are to differ depending upon the characteristics for generation-skipping tax purposes of the property that is available to satisfy them. Stated differently, this system appears appropriate to use if the instrument states a single scheme of disposition without regard to the character for generation-skipping tax purposes of the property that is available to satisfy it. When this system is appropriate, it enables the draftsperson to continue to use most of the drafting that he or she used before the advent of Chapter 13.

---

[34]See Appendix, Forms #5 and #1, *infra*.

8

Strategies To Reduce or Avoid the Tax — Part II (Planning for Transfers That Are Not Favored)

§ 8.01 USING GIFT AND ESTATE TAX BASE TO AVOID OR REDUCE TRANSFER TAX

Each property owner has the absolute ability to avoid Chapter 13 (the generation-skipping tax). The cost, of course, is involvement with Chapter 12 (the gift tax) or Chapter 11 (the estate tax). The pertinent questions are

a. When should the property owner make this decision,
b. What should the property owner (or his or her surrogate) decide, and
c. How should the property owner implement the decision?

§ 8.01(a) Inclusion in Transfer Tax Bases Rather Than in Generation-Skipping Transfers

Subject to making full use of exemptions, exclusions, and exceptions that are available with respect to the generation-skipping tax, a property owner might have an incentive to include (or, by means of powers of appointment or trustee's discretionary powers to distribute, permit one or more other persons to include) transfers in the completed gifts or gross estates of beneficiaries rather than in generation-skipping transfers at the generation levels of the beneficiaries. Except to any extent that the 5 percent surcharge of

Code Section 2001(c)(3) is applicable, inclusion of a particular transfer in a donor's completed gifts or in a decedent's gross estate never attracts more transfer tax than inclusion of the same property, instead, in a generation-skipping transfer which is fully taxable. Inclusion of property in the completed gifts or gross estate of a beneficiary requires the beneficiary to own the property or to have a general power to appoint it and, thus, in the case of outright ownership clearly requires, and in the case of the general power to appoint might require, the beneficiary to be able to control the disposition of the property and even to exhaust it.

A property owner can defer, even beyond his or her death, a decision concerning use of the completed gifts or gross estates of beneficiaries rather than generation-skipping transfers in a trust. A trustee (or a donee of a nongeneral power of appointment) who has the requisite discretion can review the permissible distributees (or appointees) and their respective transfer tax bases and can decide whether to distribute (or cause distribution of) any or all of the trust estate to one or more of them. Alternatively or additionally, if the trust permits, an independent trustee (or a donee of a nongeneral power of appointment) can grant a general power to appoint any or all of the trust estate.[1]

§ 8.01(b) Structuring Transfers To Produce a Previously-Taxed Property Credit Against Beneficiary's Estate Tax

A concept similar to avoidance of generation-skipping tax by inclusion of property in the gross estate of a beneficiary is to structure a transfer to produce a previously-taxed property credit against the estate tax that is payable with respect to the taxable estate of the beneficiary.[2]

Inclusion of the property in the gross estate of the beneficiary is not a precondition to the availability of the credit. However, the credit is not available unless the beneficiary's interest has an ascertainable value according to recognized valuation principles.[3] A sig-

---

[1]See Appendix, Form #7, *infra*.

[2]*See* Code § 2013.

[3]Treas. Reg. § 20.2013-4(a).

nificant disadvantage of a discretionary trust is that the beneficiary's interest cannot qualify for the credit.

§ 8.02 USING NONGENERAL AND TRUSTEE'S POWERS TO DEFER SKIPS

Even if a taxable transfer appears inevitable, a donee of a nongeneral power of appointment and a holder of a discretionary, fiduciary power to distribute might exercise their respective powers to defer it by appointing the property for the benefit of a non-skip person. Deferral can permit the family to use the deferred tax during the period of the deferral.

§ 8.03 USING A DISCRETIONARY DISTRIBUTION TO SKIP MORE THAN ONE GENERATION IN WHICH A PERSON HAS AN INTEREST

Distribution of property, by means of the exercise of discretion, before a taxable termination occurs with respect to it, can cause the property to skip more than one generation but produce only one generation-skipping transfer, even if a person in each skipped generation has a present interest before the distribution. Passage of the same property to the same person after a taxable termination occurs (because of other than a discretionary distribution) can subject the property to more than one generation-skipping transfer.

Assume that a property owner creates a trust to permit the trustee to pay income and principal to any one or more of the grantor's spouse and descendants (consisting of a child, a grandchild, and a great-grandchild) until the death of the survivor among the spouse, the child, and the grandchild, that the spouse has a nongeneral power exercisable during life to appoint to any one or more of the grantor's descendants and that, in default of appointment, the property will pass upon the death of the survivor to the great-grandchild if then living.

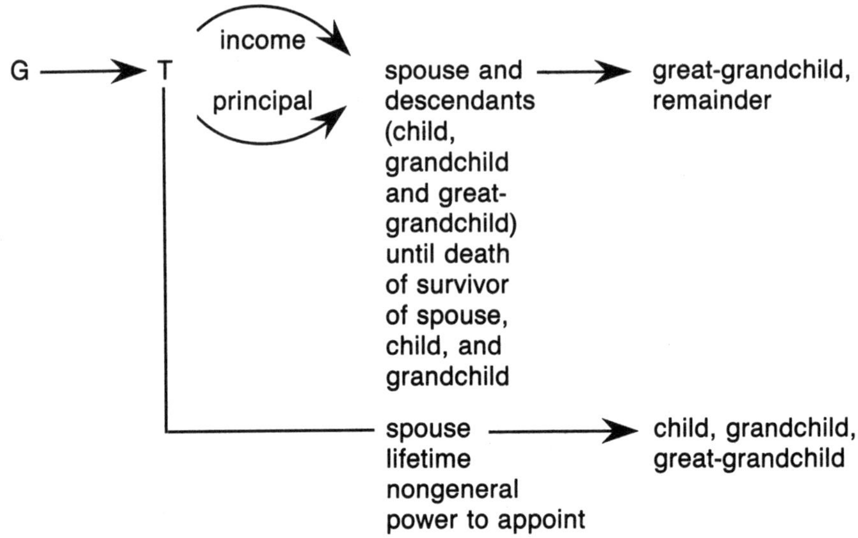

Any distribution to the grandchild before the death of the survivor of the spouse and the child and any distribution to the great-grandchild before the death of the survivor of the spouse, the child, and the grandchild, whether by means of the trustee's exercise of the power to distribute or the spouse's exercise of the power to appoint, will be a taxable transfer. According to the proposed regulations, the transfer will have the form of a taxable distribution if the distribution does not terminate all interests of the spouse and the child or of a taxable termination if the distribution does terminate all interests of the spouse and the child. If the spouse and the child predecease the grandchild and the great-grandchild, or either of them, the death of the survivor of the spouse and the child will be a taxable termination. If the grandchild survives the survivor of the spouse and the child, the great-grandchild survives the grandchild, and property passes to the great-grandchild because of the death of the grandchild, the death of the grandchild will be another taxable termination. However, passage of the property to the great-grandchild by means of a discretionary distribution before the death of the survivor of the spouse and the child (even, indeed, while the survivor is *in extremis,* in contemplation of the survivor's death) will subject the property to only one generation-skipping transfer and thus will avoid a generation-skipping transfer at the level of a generation (that is, the grandchild's) to which is assigned a person who has an interest.

§ 8.04 USING "LAYERING" (AVOIDANCE OF INTERESTS AT CERTAIN GENERATIONS) TO SKIP MORE THAN ONE GENERATION AT ONE TIME OR TO DEFER OR AVOID SKIPS

Some incentive exists to benefit one or more skip persons but to avoid creating any interest in any person in one or more generations above a particular skip person.

1. One strategy is to cause one generation-skipping transfer to skip more than one generation.
2. A second strategy is to construct transfers that effectively skip generations but that are not included in the definition of generation-skipping transfer.
3. A third strategy is to reduce the number and size of taxable terminations by providing for certain beneficiaries such amounts as the beneficiaries are expected to consume and by using either favored dispositions, such as direct skips, or the second strategy to provide (or to supplement provision) for beneficiaries assigned to lower generations. Collateral considerations tend to reinforce these incentives. The relatively smaller tax base of a direct skip compared to the tax bases of the other taxable events provides an incentive to use direct skips rather than other forms of transfers and thus reinforces the property owner's incentive to provide separately for children (and, conversely, separately for descendants other than children).

§ 8.04(a) The First Strategy — Causing a GST To Skip More than One Generation

The first strategy is a product of Chapter 13's different treatment of (i) transfers that skip the first generation below the transferor, and (ii) transfers that skip any other generation below the transferor.

A transfer that skips inclusion in the transfer tax base of an individual assigned to the generation *one below the transferor* can produce a generation-skipping transfer *regardless* of whether any individual assigned to that generation has any interest. An example that depicts a direct skip is a person's gift of $40,000 to his or her sibling's grandchild. An example that depicts a taxable distribution is a trustee's distribution of $100,000 (being one twentieth of the trust) to the grantor's grandchild during the life of the grantor's spouse from a trust that permits the trustee to pay income, or to accumulate it, and to pay principal, to either or each of the grantor's spouse and the grantor's grandchild during the life of the spouse. An example that depicts a taxable termination is the passage of the property to the grantor's grandchild upon the death of the grantor's spouse in the trust described in the preceding sentence.

However, when a transfer skips inclusion at the level of one or more generations *more than one below the transferor,* a generation-skipping transfer cannot occur at the level of any of these generations at which no individual has any interest.

Stated differently, regardless of the number of generations that a particular transfer skips and to which no individual who has any interest is assigned, only one generation-skipping tax is payable. As an example, a direct skip, by means of a direct gift, from the transferor to the transferor's great-grandchild is only one generation-skipping transfer.[4] As another example, assume that a transferor creates a trust which permits the trustee to pay income and principal to the transferor's spouse and great-grandchildren during the spouse's life, remainder to the transferor's great-grandchildren, per capita, who survive the spouse. A payment to a great-grandchild during the spouse's life will be a generation-skipping transfer but only one generation-skipping transfer. The spouse's death will be a taxable termination but only one generation-skipping transfer.

Conversely, a generation-skipping transfer additionally can occur at the level of each skipped generation more than one below the transferor and to which an individual who has an interest is assigned.

As an example, if property passes by means of a direct skip to a trust in which a grandchild has an interest immediately after the transfer, the grandchild's interest will cause the movement of the property to a great-grandchild to require two transfers rather than one.

G ⟶ T ⟶ GC life ⟶ GGC, remainder

[4]Prop. Treas. Reg. § 26.2612-1(a)(1), 57 Fed. Reg. 61361 (1992).

As another example, consider a trust that permits the trustee to pay income, or to accumulate it, and to pay principal, to any one or more among the transferor's child and the child's descendants and in which the property passes outright to a great-grandchild of the grantor after the successive terminations of the interests of the child and the child's children.

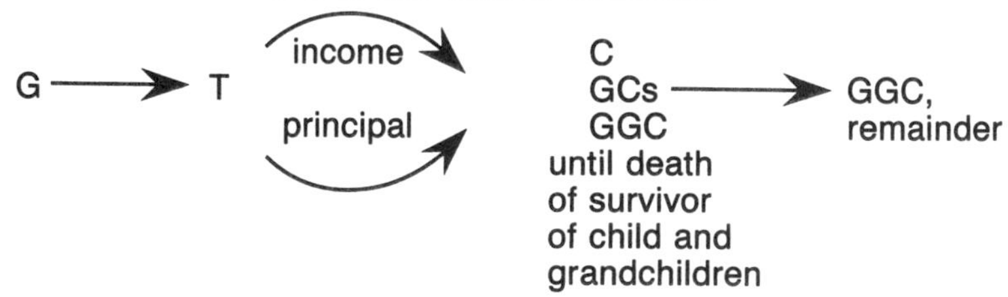

A taxable termination occurs upon the death of the child. A second taxable termination occurs upon the death of the last-surviving child of the child.

Similarly, if (i) the transfer to the trust is not a direct skip (or any other generation-skipping transfer), (ii) a non-skip person has an interest before a generation-skipping transfer occurs, (iii) a grandchild has an interest immediately after the termination of the interest of the non-skip person, and (iv) the property passes to a great-grandchild upon the termination of the interest of the grandchild after the termination of the interest of the non-skip person, the grandchild's interest will cause the movement of the property to the great-grandchild to require two transfers rather than one.

These principles provide some incentive for a wealthy person to avoid a generation-skipping transfer at the level of a particular generation by making transfers in trust or outright designed (i) so that no person with an interest is assigned to one or more consecutive generations more than one below the transferor (for example, the second below the transferor) and above a yet lower generation (for example, the third below the transferor) or (ii) if the transferor is to use a direct skip, so that no person with an interest is assigned to more than one of the consecutive generations commencing with the first below the transferor.

As an example, a property owner can avoid a transfer tax at the level of one or more generations more than one below himself or herself by (i) making transfers in which only great-grandchildren and their descendants (or, if the transfer is not to be a direct skip, only children and great-grandchildren and descendants of great-grandchildren, together) are to have interests but no grandchild is to have any interest and (ii) providing separately for grandchildren by means of transfers in which only grandchildren (or, if the transfer is not to be a direct skip, only children and grandchildren, together) are to have interests.

This incentive is different from the incentive that the Tax Reform Act of 1976 (TRA '76) provided for wealthy persons to make transfers in trust or outright designed so that no person with a present interest (or a present power) was assigned to one or more consecutive generations below the grantor commencing with the first. The TRA '76 version of Chapter 13 did not tax a transfer to a person assigned to a generation more than one below the grantor unless a person assigned to a higher generation below the grantor had a present interest (or a present power). Since, on the other hand, the TRA '86 version of Chapter 13 generally does tax a transfer to a person assigned to a generation more than one below the transferor *without regard to whether any person (for example, a child) in the generation one below the transferor has any interest,* a generation-skipping transfer generally is not avoidable by causing no person in the generation one below the transferor to have an interest.

§ 8.04(b) The Second Strategy — Constructing Transfers That Effectively Skip Generations but Are Not "Generation-Skipping Transfers"

The second strategy is a product of the definition of "skip person" and, indirectly, the definition of "taxable termination."

> A trust is a skip person with respect to a transfer only
>
> (A) if all interests in such trust are held by skip persons, or
>
> (B) if
>
> (i) there is no person holding an interest in such trust, and
>
> (ii) *at no time after such transfer may a distribution (including distributions on termination) be made from such trust to a non-skip person.* (Emphasis added.)[5]

Conversely, if no person has an interest immediately after the transfer of property into a trust and a distribution (for example, any distribution on termination) may be made from the trust to a

[5]Code § 2613(a)(2).

non-skip person after the transfer into the trust, the trust is not a skip person.

The use in the definition of taxable termination of some of the same language that appears in the definition of skip person tends to reinforce the literal meaning of the language in the definition of skip person. The function of the language in the definition of taxable termination is to create a comprehensive definition. The same language should have the same meaning each time it appears. Creation of a "gloss" upon the language in the definition of skip person would tend to undermine the definition of taxable termination.

The definition of skip person appears to provide an incentive to make transfers in trust designed so that (i) no person has an interest immediately after the transfer, (ii) a distribution (for example, a distribution on termination) *may* be made to a non-skip person after the transfer into the trust, (iii) no non-skip person in fact accedes to an interest before the property passes to a skip person, and (iv) skip persons who are assigned to at least two generations will have interests.

§ 8.04(b)(1) Deferred-Interest Model

As an example, consider a Deferred-Interest Model. A transferor creates a trust to accumulate income and not distribute principal for two years and after two years to permit the trustee to pay income, or to accumulate it, and to pay principal, to the grantor's grandchild (or to the grantor's grandchild and great-grandchild), remainder upon the death of the grandchild to the then-living descendants, per stirpes, of the grandchild or, if none, the then-living descendants, per stirpes, of the grandchild's nearest ancestor who is the grantor's child or the grantor and of whom one or more descendants then are living.

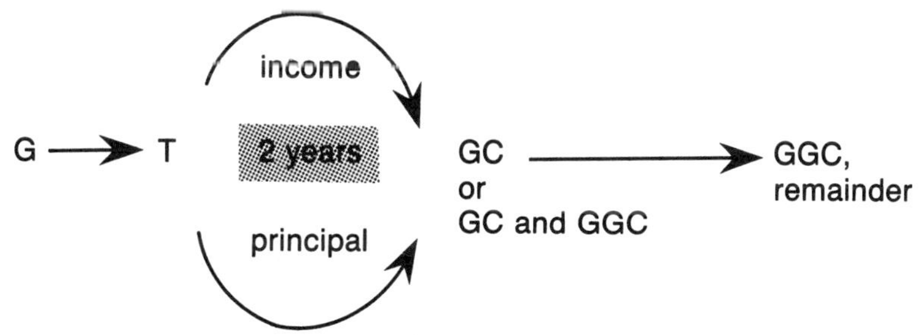

No person has an interest immediately after the grantor's transfer, and after the transfer a distribution (that is, a distribution upon termination of the trust) may be made to a non-skip person. Therefore, arguably, the trust is not a skip person. That the trust is not a skip person is sufficient, *per se,* to prevent the transfer into the trust from being a direct skip or a taxable distribution.[6] That the transfer is not from a trust is sufficient, *per se,* to prevent it from being a taxable termination.[7] Any distribution to the great-grandchild during the life of the grandchild will be to a skip person and thus will be a generation-skipping transfer, in the form (according to the proposed regulations) of a taxable distribution or, if the distribution terminates all interest of the grandchild, a taxable termination. Passage of the property to the great-grandchild upon the death of the grandchild within two years after the creation of the trust will be a taxable distribution. Passage of the property to the great-grandchild upon the death of the grandchild more than two years after the creation of the trust will be a taxable termination. Thus, the passage of the property to the great-grandchild will require only one generation-skipping transfer even though (i) the property skips two generations and (ii) a person (that is, the grandchild) assigned to one of the two generations has an interest. Whether or not a grandchild acquires an interest and whether or not the movement of the property to the great-grandchild occurs during the grandchild's life or upon the grandchild's death does not affect this result.

§ 8.04(b)(2) Movement of Property to the Great-Grandchild That Requires Two Generation-Skipping Transfers

By contrast, an interest in a grandchild immediately after the creation of the trust will tend to cause the movement of the property to the great-grandchild to require two generation-skipping transfers.

First, assume that the transfer which creates the trust is a direct skip because the grandchild has an interest immediately after the transfer and no non-skip person then has an interest.

---

[6]Code § 2612(b) and (c).

[7]Code § 2612(a).

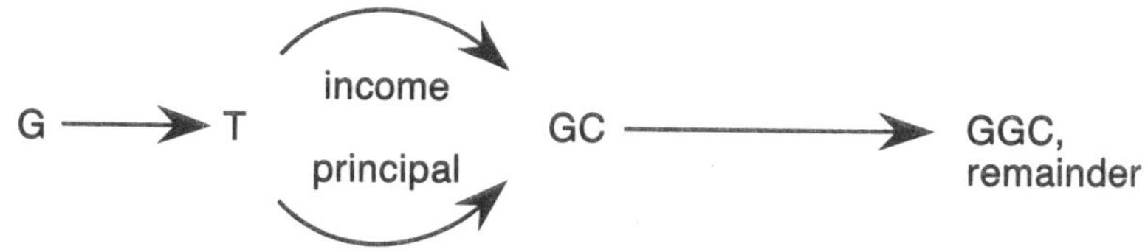

The direct skip is the first transfer, at the level of the grantor's child. The direct skip lowers the generation assignment of the transferor to the child's generation. The termination of the grandchild's interest with the great-grandchild surviving will be the second transfer, a taxable termination.

Second, assume that the transfer which creates the trust is not a generation-skipping transfer because a non-skip person (for example, the grantor's spouse or child) has an interest immediately after the transfer.

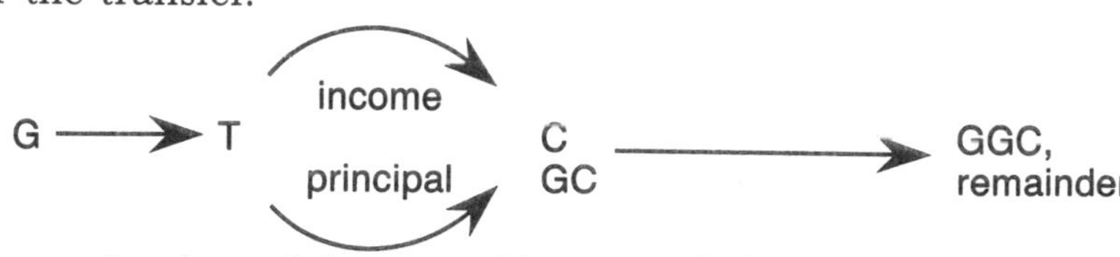

The termination of the non-skip person's interest with the grandchild surviving will be the first transfer, a taxable termination. The taxable termination of the non-skip person's interest with the grandchild surviving will lower the generation assignment of the transferor to the child's generation. The subsequent termination of the grandchild's interest with the great-grandchild surviving will be the second transfer, also a taxable termination.

§ 8.04(b)(3) A Variation of the Deferred-Interest Model

Assume, as a variation of the Deferred-Interest Model, that a non-skip person (for example, a child) has an interest at some time more than two years after the transfer which creates the trust, the non-skip person predeceases the grandchild, and the grandchild predeceases the great-grandchild.

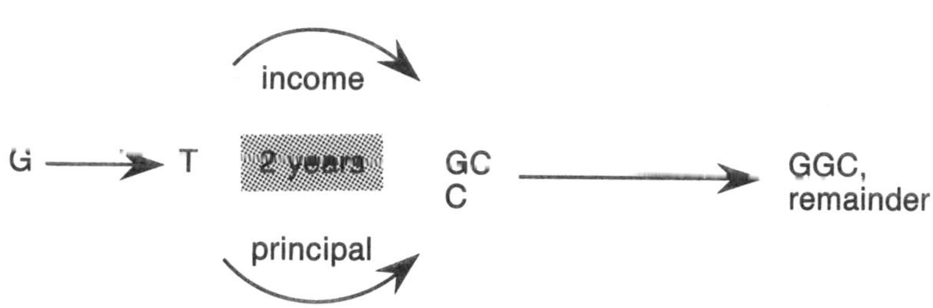

The death of the non-skip person will be a generation-skipping transfer — that is, a taxable termination. If no non-skip person were to have an interest, this generation-skipping transfer would not occur. Thus, the property owner has some incentive to use a system of layering that excludes each child from having an interest as long as a descendant assigned to a lower generation is living.

§ 8.04(c) Implementing the Strategies

How might the draftsperson implement these strategies discussed in this § 8.04?

§ 8.04(c)(1) One Arrangement for the First and the Third Strategies

One manifestation of the first and third strategies is an arrangement in which no person in one of the generations more than one below the grantor has any present interest, a person in this generation has a future interest that is designed to become a present interest at some time, and a person in a lower generation has a present interest.

Assume that a transferor creates a series of trusts, the transferor's great-grandchild has (or the transferor's great-grandchild and child have) present interests, the transferor's grandchild currently has a present interest in only one of these trusts and has a future interest in each other of these trusts, and each future interest will become a present interest at a different date (for example, upon the grandchild's attainment of a certain age) or upon the lapse of a different, fixed time after the happening of a particular event (for example, a number of days after the death of the child, in the case of the trust for the great-grandchild and child).

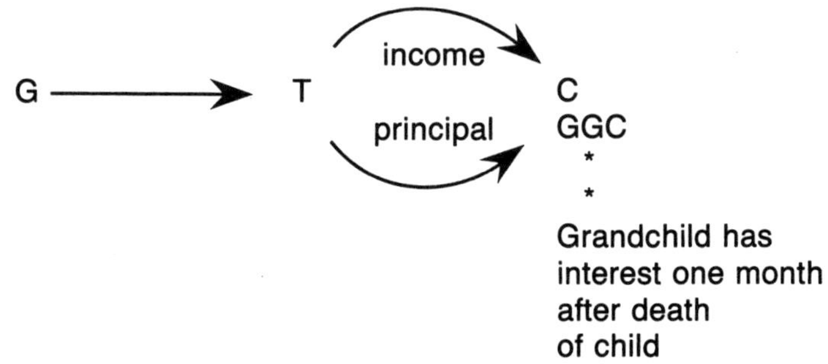

If the grandchild were to accede to an interest before the death of the child, the child were to predecease the grandchild, and the grandchild were to predecease the great-grandchild, the child's death would be a taxable termination and the grandchild's death would be another taxable termination.

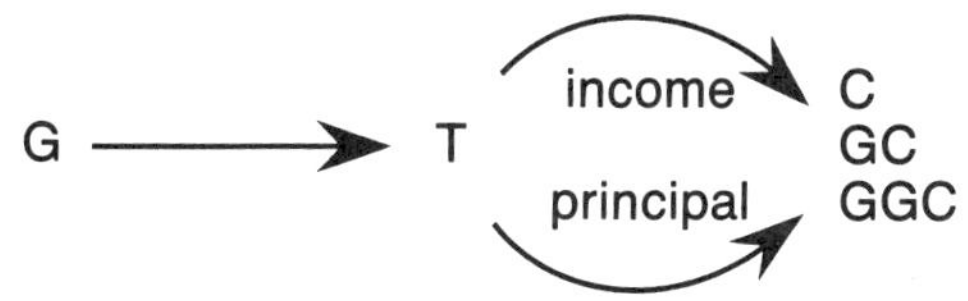

However, if the grandchild were not to accede to an interest until after some interval after the death of the child but before the death of the great-grandchild, and the great-grandchild's interest were not ignored, the child's death (that is, a taxable termination) would lower the transferor's generation to that of the grandchild and the subsequent death of the grandchild would not be a taxable termination.[8] This strategy would cause the grandchild's death at any time to be a taxable termination with respect to a limited amount of property. The termination of a future interest cannot produce a taxable termination. However, beware that an interest is not a future interest unless the contingency which prevents it is *wholly* outside the holder's control.[9] Nevertheless, if the trusts were drafted properly, a sufficient amount of property always would be available for the grandchild.

Some, but arguably not all, manifestations of this use of future interests are vulnerable to the rule that an interest (even an interest which is not "nominal") which is used "primarily" (or, according to the proposed regulations, a "significant" purpose of which is) to postpone or avoid any generation-skipping tax shall be disregarded.[10] Most vulnerable would be an arrangement in which (i) the great-grandchild received an interest only after the death of

---

[8] *See* Code § 2653(a).

[9] Former Prop. Treas. Reg. (withdrawn because of repeal of first version of Chapter 13) § 26.2613-4(d).

[10] Code § 2652(c)(2). *See also* Staff of the Joint Committee on Taxation, *Description of the Technical Corrections Act of 1988,* 364-5 (1988); Prop. Treas. Reg. § 26.2612-1(e)(2)(ii), 57 Fed. Reg. 61361 (1992).

the child and (ii) the grandchild's accession to an interest was keyed to some interval after, but by reference to, the death of the child. Less vulnerable would be an arrangement in which the great-grandchild had an interest from the creation of the trust. Yet less vulnerable would be an arrangement in which the great-grandchild had an interest from the creation of trust and in which the child never had any interest. Similarly, the keying of a grandchild's accession to an interest to the grandchild's attainment of a stated age, rather than to the death of the child, would seem to reduce vulnerability.

§ 8.04(c)(2) Using "Layered" Trusts

One comprehensive means of providing separately for persons assigned to particular generations is to use a series of "layered" trusts, with a separate trust for the benefit principally of one or more persons assigned to a single generation lower than the transferor. Although this writer principally discusses the use of this arrangement to implement the third strategy, parts or variations of this arrangement also are usable to implement the first and second strategies.

For example, for the benefit of a child (or, as the case may be, grandchild), a property owner might create a trust designed to exhaust income and principal during the child's (or, as the case may be, grandchild's) life. Perhaps the appropriate amount of corpus for this trust is the amount that might provide a sufficient amount for the child's (or, as the case may be, grandchild's) needs during his or her life. This trust can defer the imposition of generation-skipping tax upon any remaining property if, when the child (or, as the case may be, grandchild) dies, the trust benefits one or more other persons in the same generation and benefits any person assigned to a yet lower generation only after all persons in the child's (or, as the case may be, grandchild's) generation have died.

Illustration:

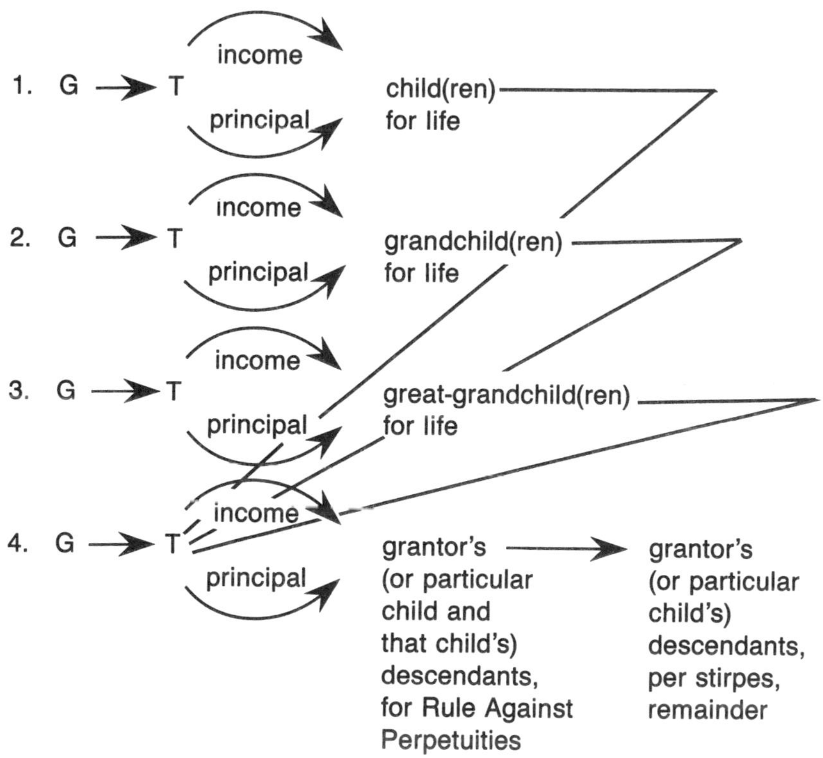

With the balance of those funds that before TRA '76 the grantor would have placed in a single generation-skipping vehicle, the grantor might establish a second (or, as the case may be, third) trust.

The second (or, as the case may be, third) trust will be for the present benefit of grandchildren (or, as the case may be, great-grandchildren) or persons assigned to a yet lower generation. However, the fiduciary might accumulate its income and not distribute principal until the grantor's descendants assigned to all higher generations die or cease being obligated to support the descendants assigned to the lower generations. By the time the descendants who are assigned to the higher generation die (or cease having the support obligations), the second (or, as the case may be, third) trust's property might approximate the amount of corpus that before TRA '76, in a "prototype" generation-skipping trust, would have been available upon the death of the grantor's child (or, as the case may be, grandchild) for the grantor's grandchildren (or, as the case may be, great-grandchildren). If the grantor is willing to permit distributions to descendants assigned to more than one generation (for example, grandchildren and great-grandchildren), the grantor can design this trust to take advantage of principles described in § 8.04(b), *supra*.

Alternatively, the grantor might enhance flexibility by reducing the size of the first and/or the second and/or the third trust and using the difference in a third (or, as the case may be, fourth), discretionary trust for all descendants. This third (or, as the case may be, fourth) trust can (but need not) have the complexion of the "main" trust described in the following § 8.04(c)(3).

§ 8.04(c)(3) Using "Main" and "Receptacle" Trusts

Another comprehensive means of layering is to use (i) one or more discretionary "main" trusts and (ii) with respect to each main trust, one or more discretionary "receptacle" trusts.

Figure 8.1, which is on the following page, is an illustration of a "wide-open" discretionary trust arrangement.

A main trust would permit the fiduciary to accumulate income or to distribute it and principal to (i) any one or more individuals included in a class (perhaps the grantor's descendants, or exclusively or primarily a particular child of the grantor and that child's descendants, living from time to time for as long as the period of any applicable Rule Against Perpetuities) and (ii) receptacle trusts created from the main trust. A single, main trust for all of the grantor's descendants tends to postpone a taxable termination but tends to bind the children (and their descendants) together financially. A separate main trust for each child and the child's descendants, rather than a single main trust for all of the grantor's

Figure 8.1

Generation-Skipping "Flow Chart"
Depicting Some Principal Features of John's Estate Plan

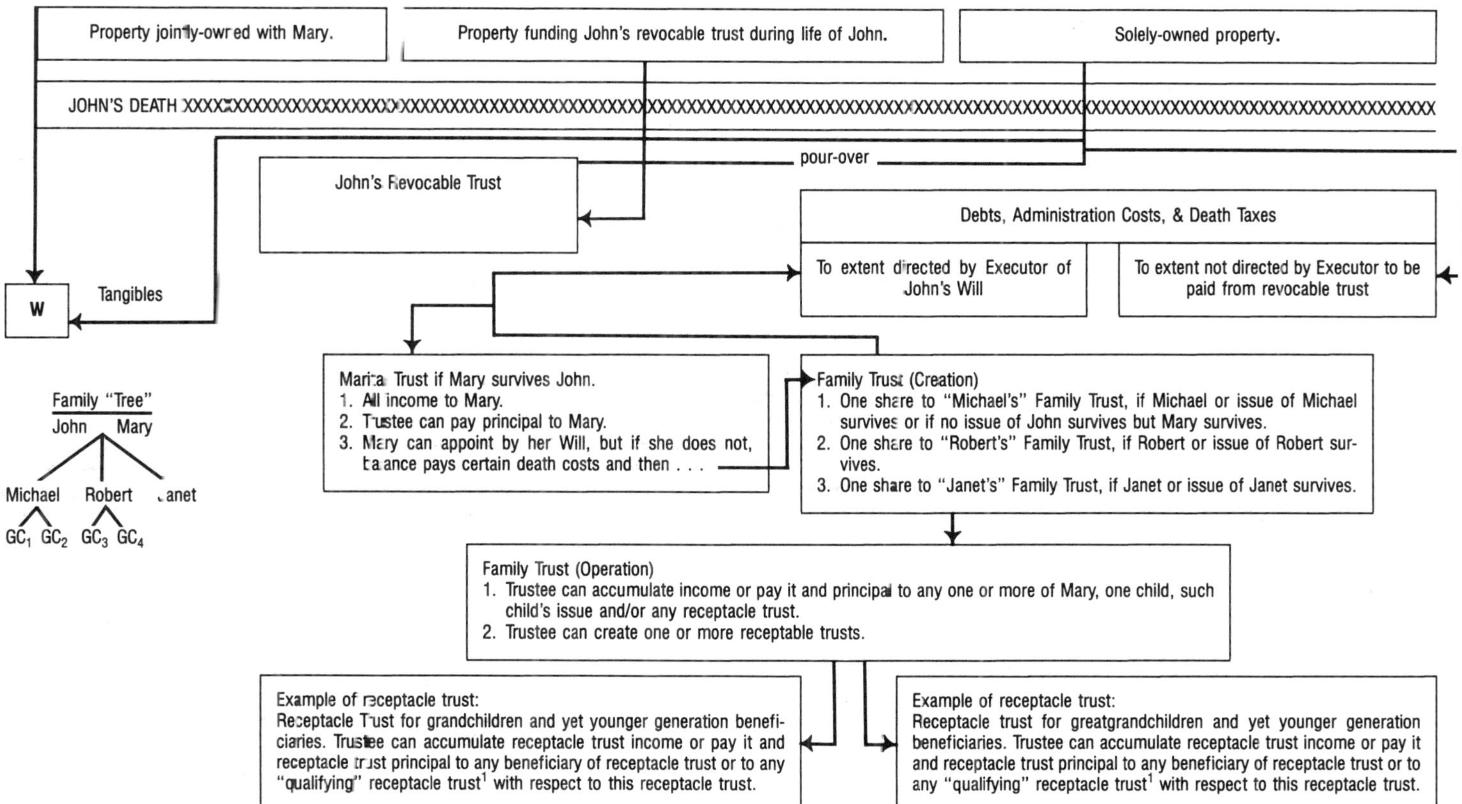

[1] A qualifying receptacle trust with respect to any particular receptacle trust is a receptacle trust that does not and cannot have any permissible distributee assigned to any generation higher than that to which is (or can be) assigned the permissible distributee of the particular receptable trust assigned to the highest generation.

descendants, does not postpone taxable terminations but permits independent financial arrangements for each child and the child's descendants.[11] A third possibility, multiple main trusts, each for the benefit of all descendants of the grantor but a separate one for the primary benefit of each child and the child's descendants, might allow both postponement of taxable terminations and independent financial arrangements for each child and the child's descendants.

Each receptacle trust also is a discretionary trust. The fiduciary of any receptacle trust can accumulate income or, except as provided in the next sentence, pay it and principal to any one or more designated individuals (who are beneficiaries of the main trust) and certain other receptacle trusts similarly established. The permissible distributees of any receptacle trust include only (i) those persons assigned to a generation no higher than a particular generation (which particular generation is specified in advance in a governing instrument that provides for the fixed creation of the receptacle trust or, alternatively, selected by the trustee upon the trustee's exercise of discretion to create a receptacle trust) and (ii) any other receptacle trust in which no individual who has an interest is (or who may have an interest will be) assigned to any generation higher than the highest generation to which any person who has an interest in the particular receptacle trust is assigned.

§ 8.04(c)(4) Distribution of Property from a Main Trust to a Receptacle Trust

A distribution of property from a main trust to a receptacle trust in which, immediately after the distribution, no non-skip person (for example, transferor's spouse or child) has an interest but a skip person has an interest is a generation-skipping transfer. However, it can skip more than one generation upon the payment of only one tax. Further, it can repose in a receptacle trust without being forced into the income, gift, or estate tax base of any individual.

A distribution from a main trust to a receptacle trust in which a non-skip person (for example, transferor's spouse or child) has an interest is not a generation-skipping transfer. A distribution from a

[11] *See* Code § 2654(b), and Former Prop. Treas. Reg. (withdrawn because of repeal of first version of Chapter 13) § 26.2613-5.

main trust to a receptacle trust in which, immediately after the distribution, no person has an interest but from which a distribution later (for example, on termination) may be made to a non-skip person is not to a skip person and, therefore, is not a taxable distribution. The distribution seems not to be to a skip person. Therefore, arguably, the distribution is not a taxable distribution and, if not a taxable termination, is not a generation-skipping transfer. At least if the distribution does not terminate all interest of each non-skip person (for example, each child) in the main trust, the distribution is not a taxable termination.[12]

If this argument prevails, the distribution effectively permits the tax-free skipping of one or more generations to which a person who has an interest is assigned.

The distribution seems to enable the trustee of the main trust to implement a "layering" system after the occurrence of the taxable transfer (for gift tax purposes or estate tax purposes) that funded the main trust. This system is to be contrasted with that which a property owner implements by means of taxable transfers (for gift tax purposes or estate tax purposes) during life or at death. A trustee's post-taxable-transfer system of layering seems able to have as much utility as a system that a property owner implements by means of taxable transfers.

---

[12]Prop. Treas. Reg. § 26.2612-1(f), Ex. 8, 57 Fed. Reg. 61362 (1992).

9

Systems of Drafting

§ 9.01 INTRODUCTION

This chapter describes what essentially are two systems of drafting that this writer has developed for his own use.[1] This writer's own drafting often includes selective use of features of one system in tandem with selective use of features of the other system.

§ 9.02 OBJECTIVES OF THE SYSTEMS

The purposes of each system are the same.

§ 9.02(a) The First Objective — Maximizing the GST Exemption

The first objective is to permit optimal use of the GST exemption of each transferor, usually each of two spouses. The overriding principle is, other things being equal, to permit maximization of the present value of the GST exemption of each transferor. Implementation of this principle requires the governing instrument to permit each of two spouses to be the transferor of a sufficient amount, allocated in such a manner as will tend to permit maximization of the present value of the tax savings that the GST exemptions can produce.

§ 9.02(b) The Second Objective — Using the Predeceased Child Exception

The second objective is to use the predeceased child exception when the failure to use it would result in a tax liability without

[1]The principles that are developed in the preceding portion of this book underlie the two systems of drafting.

accomplishing any nontax purpose or other tax purpose. Attainment of this objective requires the governing instrument to cast the transfer in the format of a direct skip. Thus, if the surviving spouse of the settlor is to have an interest in property held in a trust before the property is to pass outright to a child of a predeceased child, the governing instrument must structure the arrangement so that the surviving spouse — that is, the surviving parent of the predeceased child — and not the settlor — that is, the nonsurviving parent of the predeceased child — will be the transferor.[2]

§ 9.02(c) Decisions for Accomplishing the First Two Objectives

§ 9.02(c)(1) Selection of the Property That Will Fund Each Disposition

The most difficult aspect of accomplishing the first and second objectives is to select which transferor's property, and how much of it, shall fund each disposition. This decision determines (i) the value that the GST exemption of a particular transferor will tend to have if it is allocated to a particular disposition and (ii) the availability of the predeceased child exception. Since a person's executor cannot allocate

---

[2]Property that is included in the gross estate of the surviving spouse of the settlor cannot qualify for the predeceased child exception unless the surviving spouse is the transferor of it for generation-skipping tax purposes. This principle seems largely academic if the governing instrument provides for the creation of a QTIP trust that is to absorb any GST exemption of the predeceasing spouse that otherwise is unallocated. This QTIP trust will consist of property with respect to which the executor of the predeceased settlor (i) makes a reverse QTIP election (*see* Code Section 2652(a)(3)) and (ii) allocates GST exemption of the settlor. As a practical matter, since the only nonexempt property is property of which the surviving spouse is the transferor, only the property of which the surviving spouse is the transferor must qualify for the predeceased child exception in order to avoid tax. Generally, the executor of a predeceased spouse should make a reverse QTIP election only with respect to property (i) to which the executor will allocate GST exemption in order to avoid generation-skipping transfer tax or (ii) with respect to which the election, *per se,* will have the effect of avoiding a generation-skipping transfer. Stated differently, the executor of the predeceased spouse generally should not use the election to change the transferor with respect to any property to which the executor will not allocate GST exemption and that might produce a generation-skipping transfer.

the person's GST exemption to property of which the person is not the transferor, efficient allocation of property is a prerequisite to efficient use of the exemption. Similarly, the allocation to a particular disposition of property of which a particular person is the transferor means that the particular disposition, to that extent, cannot consist of property of which another person is the transferor. A mandate to a fiduciary to fund a particular disposition with property of which a particular person is the transferor tends to force the fiduciary to fund other dispositions with property of which another person is the transferor. This allocation is critical when property of more than one transferor — for example, the settlor and the settlor's spouse — is available to satisfy a particular disposition and the allocation of property of one will maximize the present value of the tax savings that the GST exemptions can produce but the allocation of property of the other will not. The allocation also is critical if the allocation of property of a particular transferor will, and the allocation of property of another transferor will not, cause a particular transfer to have the format of a direct skip and to qualify for the predeceased child exception.

§ 9.02(c)(2) Complexity of the Decisions

The decisions mentioned in the preceding paragraph are extremely complex. Chapter 10 analyzes them in the context of two objectives and nine combinations of formats. The combinations of formats result from grouping (i) each of three formats of shares that are set apart on a per stirpital basis with respect to a person's living children with (ii) each of the same formats of shares that are set apart on a per stirpital basis with respect to the person's deceased children for the living descendants of the deceased children. The formats are those of (a) an outright gift, (b) a gift in trust for a beneficiary until the beneficiary attains one or more ages, and (c) a gift in trust for a beneficiary for life.

§ 9.02(d) The Third Objective — Subjecting Transfers to Gift Tax or to Estate Tax Rather Than to Generation-Skipping Transfer Tax

The third objective of each system of drafting is to permit a fiduciary or other person to subject certain transfers to gift tax or to estate tax instead of subjecting them to the generation-skipping transfer tax. Generation-skipping transfers are avoided, and transfers instead are subjected to gift tax or estate tax, by means of inclusion of property in beneficiaries' gross estates for estate tax purposes or completed gifts for gift tax purposes.

§ 9.02(e) Differences Between These and Other Drafting Systems

This writer has attempted to highlight the differences between the systems that he is using and the systems that other planners apparently are using. Still, two warnings are appropriate. First, since the actual language of the governing instrument is critically important, do not assume that any feature described in this material is the same as, or similar to, any feature, whether or not similarly described, of any system that is not explicitly described in this material. Second, this writer believes that a significant portion of the other drafting of which he has knowledge is ill-conceived to accomplish the objectives.

§ 9.03 TWO DRAFTING SYSTEMS

§ 9.03(a) "Discretionary System of Drafting"

This writer uses the term "discretionary system of drafting" to describe a system by which the governing instrument permits, rather than requires, configurations that permit attainment of the objectives. This type of system allows the discretion of a power holder (other than the person who creates the governing instrument) to determine the relative sizes of dispositions that are, and are not, intended to be subject to the generation-skipping transfer tax. Presumably, the power holder will exercise this type of discretion to create one or more dispositions that are intended to have inclusion ratios of zero and one or more dispositions that are intended to have inclusion ratios of one. If the dispositions that are, and are not, to be subject to the tax are identical except for size, exercise of the discretion will not alter beneficial enjoyment. Conversely, substantive differences between these dispositions can cause exercise of the discretion to affect beneficial enjoyment.

§ 9.03(b) "Mandatory System of Drafting"

This writer uses the term "mandatory system of drafting" to describe a system by which the governing instrument requires, rather than permits, configurations that are designed to attain the objectives. This type of system causes the sizes of one or more dispositions to equal the amount of a transferor's GST exemption that is unallocated before the transferor's death. Contrary to other drafting with which this writer is familiar, this writer's mandatory system does *not* cause these sizes to depend upon (i) actual allocation of any GST exemption after the governing instrument becomes irrevocable (that is, usually, after the transferor's death) or (ii) any other exercise of discretion.

§ 9.03(c) Pseudo-Mandatory Systems

Any system which mandates that the sizes of particular dispositions shall vary with the amount of GST exemption which an executor actually allocates depends, ultimately, upon a power holder's exercise of discretion. Therefore, to this extent, this type of system is only superficially mandatory, actually is discretionary, and is susceptible to arguments about efficacy that apply to certain aspects of a system that explicitly is discretionary. These pseudo-mandatory systems apparently are being used widely.

Subject to any equitable adjustments that are required, an executor's discretion to allocate GST exemption is always, in any system, an ability to affect beneficial enjoyment by determining whether a particular disposition shall, or shall not, generate liability for tax and, therefore, how much shall benefit the family and how much shall benefit the Internal Revenue Service. However, an executor's discretion directly to determine the size of a particular disposition because the governing instrument defines the size of the disposition in terms of the amount of the GST exemption that the executor actually allocates to it or to one or more other dispositions is a disguised, additional ability to alter beneficial enjoyment. This writer prefers to cast in traditional formats, subject to traditional guides and constraints, any ability so significantly to affect enjoyment. This preference is particularly strong when the fiduciary has a beneficial interest in his or her decisions.

§ 9.03(d) Dealing with an Executor's Failure To Allocate as Anticipated

If the transferor's executor fails to allocate GST exemption as the settlor of the governing instrument anticipated and the governing instrument does not include a procedure to address the problem, this writer's manner of mandating relative sizes will produce a disposition that is intended to, but will not, have an inclusion ratio of zero. This problem is a product of a mandate. Inclusion, even in an instrument in which the mandate appears, of discretion to split a single trust into two or more trusts might afford a solution. If an executor that wishes to allocate a less-than-anticipated amount of GST exemption to a particular disposition will inform the trustee, in advance, about how much the executor actually will allocate, the trustee can split the disposition into (i) a part that will absorb the exemption that the executor actually will allocate and (ii) a part that will consist of the excess. If the executor will cooperate to the extent of allocating the exemption solely to the first part, the first part should have an inclusion ratio of zero, and the second part should have an inclusion ratio of one. However, of course, this procedure will not assure that substantively a disposition that the settlor intended to be GST-exempt will make good sense if in fact it is nonexempt because an executor failed to allocate GST exemption as the settlor anticipated.

§ 9.03(e) Planning for Use of a Spouse's GST Exemption

Anticipation is particularly unreliable when it concerns whether and how a surviving spouse will use his or her own GST exemption with respect to property of which he or she is the transferor but that passes according to a governing instrument that the predeceasing spouse created. The actual use of the GST exemption of the surviving spouse depends upon the exercise of discretion by the spouse or by a fiduciary who owes no duty to the predeceasing spouse. The relationship between (i) the creation of a disposition of a particular size that is related to the GST exemption that a settlor hopes the transferor's executor will allocate to it and (ii) the actual allocation of the exemption as the settlor desired is tenuous even when the executor of the settlor is the party that is to make the actual allocation. It is even more tenuous when the GST exemption in question is not that of the person who created the governing instrument. Stated differently, this writer prefers not to rely upon a person (or a person's executor) allocating the person's GST exemption to property that is the subject of a disposition that passes under a governing instrument that another person created rather than to property that is the subject of a disposition that the owner of the exemption created. Accordingly, this writer prefers not to mandate that the size of any disposition under the governing instrument that one spouse created shall depend upon the GST exemption of the other spouse (i) which is unallocated before the other spouse's death or (ii) which the executor of the other spouse actually allocates to property which passes under the governing instrument. However, if (i) upon any contingency either spouse has insufficient property with which to create the desired dispositions according to his or her own dispositive instrument and (ii) the dispositions that are intended to be GST-exempt differ substantively from those that are not intended to be GST-exempt, the creator of the governing instrument must cause the size of a disposition to depend at least on the availability of the other spouse's GST exemption. This writer addresses this situation by mandating that the size of a disposition which one spouse creates with the intention that it shall have an inclusion ratio of zero but of which the other spouse is the transferor shall depend upon the extent to which the other spouse's GST exemption which is unallocated before the other spouse's death exceeds that which would eliminate generation-skipping tax upon all transfers of all other property of which the other spouse is the transferor.

§ 9.03(f) Effect of Permission To Consolidate Dispositions

Permission in a governing instrument for a fiduciary freely to consolidate dispositions that substantively are similar is another method of transforming what nominally is a mandatory system into a discretionary system. This permission might cause the system to become susceptible to arguments about efficacy that apply to certain aspects of a system that explicitly is discretionary.

§ 9.03(g) Appropriateness of Using the Discretionary and Mandatory Systems

The aspect of the discretionary system that governs the relative sizes of dispositions is inappropriate to use unless the dispositions that the governing instrument creates do not differ substantively depending upon whether they are, or are not, subject to the generation-skipping transfer tax. Conversely, whenever the dispositions that are, and are not, intended to be subject to generation-skipping transfer tax are substantively identical, the feature of the mandatory system that mandates the sizes of the dispositions arguably can create an instrument that is unnecessarily complex and rigid and capable of producing uneconomically small trusts. However, a counterargument is that this feature of a mandatory system is necessary *even if* the dispositions which are, and are not, intended to be subject to the tax are substantively identical. According to the counterargument, the exercise of discretion to attempt to create shares of which one person rather than another is the transferor (and, hence, to allow allocation of the unused GST exemption of a particular transferor and to cause the transfer of a particular share to assume the format of a direct skip and thus qualify for the predeceased child exception) will not cause any share to consist of other than a pro rata portion of whatever property the fiduciary can — that is, not does — allocate to it. The discretionary selection of property (and, hence, of the transferor of it) produces this concern with respect both to allocation of GST exemption and creation of the format of a direct skip. This aspect of the discretionary system has the disadvantage of producing more uncertainty than its mandatory counterpart about accomplishment of some of the objectives. The proposed regulations, in fact, would impose a rule of refusing to recognize, for purposes of the generation-skipping tax, the discretionary severance of any trust that is not included in the gross estate of the transferor or that is split with the economic effect of fractional shares but without pro rata allocation of each and every asset.

§ 9.03(h) Comparison of Governing Instruments — Before and After Advent of Generation-Skipping Tax

Compared to the drafting of governing instruments before the advent of the generation-skipping transfer tax, the discretionary system requires only the addition of authority for (i) non-pro rata distribution of various funds (not merely non-pro rata distribution of various assets of a single fund) and (ii) the creation of separate trusts, identical to each other, to serve as receptacles for property with differing tax characteristics. The mandatory system, on the other hand, requires governing instruments that differ markedly from instruments that were appropriate before the generation-skipping transfer tax.

§ 9.04 ANALYSIS OF A TYPICAL GOVERNING INSTRUMENT AT CRITICAL PHASES

The method of the analysis that follows is to view a typical instrument at critical phases, to illustrate how each system of drafting applies, and to evaluate each system and combinations of the two.

§ 9.04(a) Size of Marital Disposition

Description of Disposition	Discretionary System of Drafting	Mandatory System of Drafting
Size of Marital Disposition	The governing instrument creates the smallest marital disposition necessary to cause the taxable estate to equal the largest amount with respect to which no estate tax is payable. The surviving spouse (by disclaiming the marital disposition and receiving the same or similar beneficial enjoyment from a disclaimer trust) and the settlor's executor (by making a partial QTIP election) can increase the taxable estate to such size as can absorb the settlor's GST exemption unallocated before the settlor's death.	The governing instrument creates either (i) the smallest marital disposition necessary to cause the taxable estate to equal the largest amount with respect to which no estate tax is payable or (ii) a marital disposition of what remains after creation of a nonmarital trust of such size as can absorb the settlor's GST exemption unallocated before the settlor's death.

§ 9.04(b) Format(s) of Marital Disposition

Description of Disposition	Discretionary System of Drafting	Mandatory System of Drafting
(1) QTIP Trust	The governing instrument provides for one QTIP trust. The trustee exercises discretion to split it into two QTIP trusts.[3] The first consists of such amount as, together with such of the nonmarital disposition as can produce any generation-skipping transfer, can absorb the settlor's GST exemption unallocated before the settlor's death. The second consists of the balance. The settlor's executor elects for generation-skipping tax purposes to ignore the QTIP election for the first QTIP trust and allocates GST exemption to it.	The governing instrument mandates the creation of two QTIP trusts.[4] They are denominated Marital Trust #1 and Marital Trust #2. Marital Trust #1 consists of such amount as, together with such of the nonmarital disposition as can produce any generation-skipping transfer, can absorb the settlor's GST exemption unallocated before the settlor's death. Marital Trust #2 consists of the balance. The settlor's executor elects for generation-skipping tax purposes to ignore the QTIP election for Marital Trust #1 and allocates GST exemption to it.

[3] See Appendix, Form #1, *infra*.

[4] See Appendix, Form #2, *infra*.

(2) QTIP Trust/Right-To-Withdraw Trust	Not applicable.	The governing instrument mandates the creation of two marital trusts. They are denominated Marital Trust #1 and Marital Trust #2. Marital Trust #1 is a QTIP trust. It consists of such amount as, together with such of the nonmarital disposition as can produce any generation-skipping transfer, can absorb the settlor's GST exemption unallocated before the settlor's death. Marital Trust #2 consists of the balance. The surviving spouse can withdraw any or all of Marital Trust #2 at any time.[5] The settlor's executor elects for generation-skipping tax purposes to ignore the QTIP election for Marital Trust #1 and allocates GST exemption to it.
(3) Right-To-Withdraw Trust	The governing instrument provides for one marital trust as to which the surviving spouse can withdraw any or all at any time. The surviving spouse disclaims such part of it as consists of such amount as, together with such of the nonmarital disposition as can produce any generation-skipping transfer, can absorb the settlor's GST exemption unallocated before the settlor's death. According to the governing instrument, the property thus disclaimed passes into a disclaimer trust. The settlor's executor elects to treat the disclaimer trust as QTIP, elects for generation-skipping tax purposes to ignore the QTIP election of the disclaimer trust, and allocates GST exemption to the disclaimer trust.	Not applicable.

Comment

The marital arrangement that imposes the least constraints is a trust from which the surviving spouse can withdraw all principal at any time. The mandatory system requires the creation of a QTIP trust that has a value equal to the amount (if any) by which the settlor's GST exemption unallocated before the settlor's death exceeds the amount of the nonmarital disposition that can generate liability for generation-skipping tax. Thus, the mandatory system is inconsistent with a marital disposition that wholly is a right-to-withdraw trust. If (i) the settlor's gross estate minus debts and costs of administration might not exceed the amount that the settlor's

---

[5]See Appendix, Form #3, *infra*.

unified credit can shelter by an amount that justifies the inclusion of the excess in a separate trust or (ii) the settlor wants to allow the settlor's surviving spouse to determine whether to impose any constraints, the use of the discretionary system to create a right-to-withdraw trust and to permit a QTIP disclaimer trust is preferable to a marital arrangement that mandatorily is to consist of one or more QTIP trusts.

§ 9.04(c) Marital Disposition During Life of Surviving Spouse

Description of Disposition	Discretionary System of Drafting	Mandatory System of Drafting
(1) QTIP Trust	The trustee exercises discretion to exhaust the GST-nonexempt trust before the trustee invades principal of the GST-exempt trust.	The governing instrument requires the trustee to exhaust Marital Trust #2 (*i.e.*, the trust that is anticipated to be GST-nonexempt, at least until the death of the surviving spouse) before the trustee invades principal of Marital Trust #1 (*i.e.*, the trust that is anticipated to be GST-exempt).[6]
(2) QTIP Trust/Right-To-Withdraw Trust	Not applicable.	The governing instrument requires the trustee to exhaust Marital Trust #2 (*i.e.*, the trust that is anticipated to be GST-nonexempt, at least until the death of the surviving spouse) before the trustee invades principal of Marital Trust #1 (*i.e.*, the trust that is anticipated to be GST-exempt).[7]
(3) Right-To-Withdraw Trust	The trustee exercises discretion to exhaust the GST-nonexempt trust (*i.e.*, the right-to-withdraw trust) before the trustee invades principal of the GST-exempt trust (*i.e.*, the QTIP trust).	Not applicable.

§ 9.04(d) Size of Nonmarital Disposition upon Death of Predeceasing Spouse

Description of Disposition	Discretionary System of Drafting	Mandatory System of Drafting
Size of Nonmarital Disposition upon Death of Predeceasing Spouse	The nonmarital disposition consists of the credit shelter amount or, if the settlor's executor makes a partial QTIP election or the surviving spouse disclaims a portion of the marital disposition (and no QTIP election pertains to it), a greater amount.	The nonmarital disposition consists either of (i) the amount that the unified credit can shelter or (ii) an amount equal to the settlor's GST exemption unallocated before the settlor's death.

[6] See Appendix, Form #2, *infra*.

[7] See Appendix, Form #3, *infra*.

§ 9.04(e) Marital Disposition upon Death of Surviving Spouse

Description of Disposition	Discretionary System of Drafting	Mandatory System of Drafting
Marital Disposition upon Death of Surviving Spouse	The governing instrument (by means of a trust provision which directs that the marital trust of which the surviving spouse is the transferor shall bear all death taxes payable upon the death of the surviving spouse with respect to all marital trusts) or the surviving spouse (by means of (i) a waiver of apportionment and a right of reimbursement, (ii) a disclaimer of the right to have the disclaimer trust pay taxes with respect to itself, or (iii) the exercise of a power of appointment with respect to property that the spouse has not disclaimed) exonerates the marital trust which is GST-exempt from bearing death taxes payable upon the death of the surviving spouse. The governing instrument adds the marital disposition to the nonmarital disposition in default of the surviving spouse's exercise of a power of appointment.	The governing instrument mandates the payment from Marital Trust #2 (*i.e.*, the trust that is anticipated to be GST-nonexempt, at least until the death of the surviving spouse) of all death taxes payable upon the death of the surviving spouse with respect to Marital Trust #1 (*i.e.*, the trust that is anticipated to GST-exempt) and Marital Trust #2, in default of the surviving spouse's exercise of a power of appointment.[8] The governing instrument adds the marital disposition to the nonmarital disposition in default of the surviving spouse's exercise of a power of appointment and mandates the segregation and separate disposition of (i) Marital Trust #1, the credit shelter trust, and any of Marital Trust #2 that the GST exemption of the spouse could exempt if the exemption first were allocated to all other property of which the spouse is the transferor, on the one hand, and (ii) any balance of Marital Trust #2, on the other.

§ 9.04(f) Formats of Nonmarital Disposition upon Death of Surviving Spouse

Description of Disposition	Discretionary System of Drafting	Mandatory System of Drafting
(1) If Settlor Is the Survivor	The trustee exercises discretion to split a trust into two trusts.[9] One consists of property with a value equal to the settlor's GST exemption unallocated before the settlor's death. The second consists of the balance. The settlor's executor allocates the settlor's GST exemption to the first.	The governing instrument creates two trusts.[10] One consists of a fractional portion with a numerator equal to the settlor's GST exemption unallocated before the settlor's death. The second consists of the balance. The settlor's executor allocates the settlor's GST exemption to the first. The governing instrument mandates non-pro rata allocation of the two trusts, to permit optimal use of the settlor's GST exemption and, by casting transfers in the format of direct skips, the predeceased child exemption, according to principles similar to those discussed in § 10.02, Table 1, *infra.*.

---

[8]See Appendix, Forms #2 and #3, *infra*.

[9]See Appendix, Form #1, *infra*.

[10]See Appendix, Form #4, *infra*.

Comment

The mandatory system is necessary if the portion of the nonmarital disposition that exceeds the transferor's unallocated GST exemption is to differ substantively from the portion that does not exceed the transferor's unallocated GST exemption. Conversely, if the portion of the nonmarital disposition that exceeds the transferor's unallocated GST exemption is not to differ substantively from the portion of it that does not exceed the transferor's unallocated GST exemption, the discretionary system seems more flexible.

Description of Disposition	Discretionary System of Drafting	Mandatory System of Drafting
(2) If Settlor's Spouse Is the Survivor	The trustee's exercise of discretion or the surviving spouse's exercise of a nongeneral power of appointment causes non-pro rata allocation of (i) property of which the settlor is the transferor (to permit use of the settlor's GST exemption) and (ii) property of which the surviving spouse is the transferor (to cast a transfer in the format of a direct skip, use the predeceased child exception, and permit use of the spouse's GST exemption), according to the principles discussed in § 10.02, Table I, *infra.*.[11]	The governing instrument mandates non-pro rata allocation of (i) property of which the settlor is the transferor and which is anticipated to be exempt (that is, Marital Trust #1 and the credit shelter trust) and property of which the spouse is the transferor and which is anticipated to be exempt (that is, any of Martial Trust #2 that the GST exemption of the spouse could exempt if the spouse's exemption first were allocated to all other property of which the spouse is the transferor), (ii) other property of which the settlor is the transferor, and (iii) other property of which the spouse is the transferor (that is, any balance of Marital Trust #2), according to the principles discussed in § 10.02, Table I, *infra.*[12]

Comment

The function of these allocations is to place the properties of which different persons are transferors in such configurations as will (i) provide optimal use of the predeceased child exception and (ii) permit the transferor's executor to allocate GST exemption in such a manner as maximizes the present value of the tax that the exemption can save. The discretionary system relies on non-pro rata distributions (i) to allocate exempt property of a particular transferor to a particular disposition and not to another and (ii) to control the identity of the transferor by allocating property of which one spouse, rather than the other, is the transferor. The

[11] See Appendix, Form #5, *infra.*

[12] See Appendix, Form #6, *infra.*

ability of the discretionary system to accomplish either function is uncertain. Conceivably, only the mandatory system can accomplish these objectives. The draftsperson might consider including the mandatory system and, depending upon how the law develops, (i) using the mandatory procedures or (ii) foregoing the mandatory procedures and using discretion (by a donee's exercise of a nongeneral power of appointment) instead. Inclusion of a nongeneral power of appointment will not prevent implementation of a mandate and will permit use of discretion.

Description of Disposition	Discretionary System of Drafting	Mandatory System of Drafting
(3) Features **(a)** Inclusion of GST-nonexempt Property in Beneficiary's Gross Estate or Gift Tax Base	The governing instrument permits inclusion of property in a beneficiary's gross estate by one or more of (i) the trustee's distribution of the property to the beneficiary, (ii) a donee's exercise of a nongeneral power of appointment to distribute the property to the beneficiary, (iii) a donee's exercise of a nongeneral power of appointment to grant a presently exercisable general power to appoint the property (and, thus, to include the property in the gross estate of the donee of the nongeneral power by invoking what is known as the Delaware Tax Trap — *see* Code § 2041(a)(3)), and (iv) an independent trustee's grant to the beneficiary of a general power to appoint the property.[13]	The governing instrument vests, for estate tax purposes, all or a formula-determined portion of such property as exceeds the property that will be exempt if the transferor's unallocated GST exemption is allocated to it.

Comment

As concerns the objective of providing efficiently and flexibly for inclusion of property in, or exclusion of property from, a beneficiary's gross estate, this writer regards the mandatory system as extremely rigid. He believes that this decision about including property in a beneficiary's gross estate in order to avoid a generation-skipping transfer is inappropriate to make irrevocably until the transfer (for example, the death of the beneficiary) is imminent. The mandatory system violates this principle. It requires a determination when the governing instrument becomes irrevocable.

---

[13]See Appendix, Form #7, *infra*.

Description of Disposition	Discretionary System of Drafting	Mandatory System of Drafting
(b) Beneficiary's Partial Right To Withdraw from Continuing Trust	The trustee exercises discretion to split each trust for a descendant into two trusts.[14] One has an inclusion ratio of zero. The other has an inclusion ratio of one. The trustee exercises discretion to make non-pro rata allocations, thus causing the descendant's right(s) to withdraw to coincide to the extent possible with the trust that has an inclusion ratio of one.[15]	The governing instrument mandates the creation of two trusts for each descendant. One has an inclusion ratio of zero. The other has an inclusion ratio of one. The governing instrument provides that the right to withdraw applies to the trust with the higher inclusion ratio.

Comment

The efficacy of this aspect of the discretionary system is unclear. The mandatory system can create a series of trusts that are uneconomically small. A hybrid system, combining (i) the discretionary creation of two sets of trusts and (ii) the mandatory application of the rights to withdraw to property that has the highest inclusion ratio, might solve these problems and also offer a better chance than the discretionary system of accomplishing the objective.[16] Conceivably, however, any exercise of discretion that causes the trusts to differ substantively from each other can prevent recognition of the severance for puposes of the generation-skipping tax.[17]

---

[14]See Appendix, Form #1, *infra.*

[15]See Appendix, Form #5, *infra.*

[16]See Appendix, Form #8, *infra.*

[17]*See* Prop. Treas. Reg. § 26.2654-1(c), 57 Fed. Reg. 61371 (1992).

10

Allocation of Property Among Shares of Living and Deceased Children: Solutions for Drafting and Administration

§ 10.01 INTRODUCTION

This chapter explores the optimal allocation of property to shares that parents set apart at the death of the survivor of them with respect to their children, living and deceased. Table I analyzes the allocation of (i) property to which GST exemption of the parents is allocable, (ii) property of the predeceasing parent in excess of that to which GST exemption is allocable, and (iii) property of the surviving parent in excess of that to which GST exemption is allocable. It uses the structure of the nine combinations of formats that result from grouping (i) each of three formats of shares that are set apart with respect to living children with (ii) each of the same formats of shares that are set apart with respect to children for the living descendants of the deceased children. As stated in § 9.02(c)(2), *supra,* the formats are those of (a) an outright gift, (b) a gift in trust for a beneficiary until the beneficiary attains one or more ages and (c) a gift in trust for a beneficiary for life.

Each format is analyzed in the context of two objectives. The first objective is that actuarial probability is the dominant criterion. This means that the property owner is willing to seek a probable saving of tax even if the failure to receive the saving will cause the shares to deviate from a strict per stirpital allocation at the level of a generation below that of children. The first objective is assumed in Column (1). The second objective is that maintenance of per stirpital allocation is the dominant criterion. This means that the property owner is willing to forego tax savings that are probable, but not certain, in order to maintain per stirpital allocation at the level of each generation. The second objective is assumed in Column (2). The forms to which the drafting solutions refer follow the respective formats in § 10.03, *infra*.

The analysis is complex. Different analysts might draw different conclusions from the same or similar facts. The objectives are somewhat arbitrary. A property owner might change between them, abandon them, or seek a combination of them and others. The formats also are somewhat arbitrary, especially when a share for one descendant in a given generation has one format and another share for another descendant in the same generation has another. While the objectives and the formats promote analysis, their nature suggests that flexibility is important.

Each "action solution" specifies at the time of an allocation how the allocation is to occur at that time. Each "drafting solution" specifies at one time (namely, the execution of the governing instrument) how an allocation is to occur at a later time.

One method is to grant discretion to a fiduciary to allocate property among the shares in such manner as the fiduciary deems best. This method presents questions about whether the Internal Revenue Service will honor the results for tax purposes. This method offers apparent flexibility. However, fiduciary duties might make the discretion more illusory than real.

Another method is to mandate the fiduciary to allocate property with particular characteristics to particular shares. This method has the disadvantage of inflexibility. However, arguably, it has the advantage of producing results that the Internal Revenue Service and the beneficiaries most likely must accept.

Given the nature of the classifications and the objectives, a system that uses a mandate but takes into account all events that occurred before the allocation date seems appealing. Arguably, the drafting system of choice is to mandate a tax result (rather than to mandate a specific allocation) and, by implication, to mandate whatever allocation produces the tax result at the time as of which the allocation is to occur. Form A exemplifies this approach. This method always is applicable.

§ 10.02 THE FORMATS, DRAFTING SOLUTIONS, AND DRAFTING COMMENTS

TABLE I

Optimal Allocation of Property to Shares for Descendants, Per Stirpes

	(1) Assuming that actuarial probability is the dominant criterion		(2) Assuming that maintenance of per stirpal allocation is the dominant criterion	
	Considerations*		Considerations*	
Format**	(a)	(b)	(a)	(b)
Respective formats of (i) shares set apart with respect to deceased children and (ii) shares set apart with respect to living children	Optimal allocation of (i) GST-exempt or exemptible property, (ii) excess (nonexemptible) property of which predeceasing spouse is transferor and (iii) excess (nonexemptible) property of which surviving spouse is transferor	Relative importance of eliminating GST vulnerability of (i) shares set apart with respect to deceased children and (ii) shares set apart with respect to living children	Optimal allocation of (i) GST-exempt or exemptible property, (ii) excess (nonexemptible) property of which predeceasing spouse is transferor and (iii) excess (nonexemptible) property of which surviving spouse is transferor	Relative importance of eliminating GST vulnerability of (i) shares set apart with respect to deceased children and (ii) shares set apart with respect to living children

*Use this material by selecting the formats that the settlor would select if the subject property were GST-exempt; provided, *if* (but only if) the dominant objective of the settlor in the event a child were to predecease the survivor of the settlor and the settlor's spouse would be to maximize the property that could benefit the children (as opposed to descendants in lower generations) of the deceased child, select the format of an outright gift or a trust for ages for each disposition from each share that is set apart with respect to a deceased child.

**A donee of a testamentary, nongeneral power of appointment who dies during the existence of a trust for his or her benefit can change the format of his or her share.

	(1)		(2)	
	(a)	(b)	(a)	(b)
Case A (i) Outright; (ii) Outright	Predeceased child exception and GST exemption are equally effective when applied to outright disposition of shares set apart with respect to deceased children.	Elimination of GST vulnerability is important *only* for shares set apart with respect to deceased children.	Predeceased child exception and GST exemption are equally effective when applied to outright disposition of shares set apart with respect to deceased children.	Elimination of GST vulnerability is important *only* for shares set apart with respect to deceased children.

Action and Drafting Solution (applicable to **(1)** and **(2)**): Allocate to the shares that are set apart with respect to deceased children property that is GST-exempt or exemptible or, if the division into shares occurs upon the death of the surviving spouse, (i) property that is GST-exempt or exemptible and (ii) other property of which the surviving spouse is the transferor. See § 10.03, Form #B, *infra*.

	(1)		(2)	
	(a)	**(b)**	**(a)**	**(b)**
Case B (i) Outright; (ii) Trust for life	Predeceased child exception avoids generation-skipping transfer for shares set apart with respect to deceased children and does not apply to shares set apart with respect to living children. Subject to eliminating GST involvement for each share equally except to any extent that a benefit to one share does not produce a detriment to another, attempt to use (i) GST exemption (*i.e.*, allocate property of which each spouse is transferor, to extent of each's GST exemption) for shares set apart with respect to living children and (ii) predeceased child exception (*i.e.*, allocate property of which surviving spouse is transferor in excess of that to which GST exemption is allocable) for shares set apart with respect to deceased children.	Equal importance.	Predeceased child exception avoids generation-skipping transfer for shares set apart with respect to deceased children and does not apply to shares set apart with respect to living children. Subject to eliminating GST involvement for each share equally except to any extent that a benefit to one share does not produce a detriment to another, attempt to use (i) GST exemption (*i.e.*, allocate property of which each spouse is transferor, to extent of each's GST exemption) for shares set apart with respect to living children and (ii) predeceased child exception (*i.e.*, allocate property of which surviving spouse is transferor in excess of that to which GST exemption is allocable) for shares set apart with respect to deceased children.	Equal importance.

Action and Drafting Solution (applicable to **(1)** and **(2)**): First, if the division into shares occurs upon the death of the surviving spouse, allocate pro rata to each share that is set apart with respect to a deceased child property of which the surviving spouse is the transferor in excess of that to which GST exemption is allocable. Second, allocate exempt or exemptible property of which each spouse is the transferor pro rata to each share that is set apart with respect to a living child, to the extent of the amount allocable to any share according to the preceding sentence. Third, allocate any remaining property pro rata to any balance of each share. See § 10.03, Form #C, *infra*.

Comment re Drafting Solution (applicable to **(1)** and **(2)**): Step Third requires pro rata allocation. This allocation seems possible without drafting.

	(1)		(2)	
	(a)	(b)	(a)	(b)
Case C (i) Outright; (ii) Trust for ages	Predeceased child exception avoids generation-skipping transfer for shares set apart with respect to deceased children and does not apply to shares set apart with respect to living children. Unlike Case A, allocation of GST exemption to shares set apart with respect to living children has some utility. However, unlike Case B, because a share set apart with respect to a living child probably will pass outright to the child, it has a lower priority than allocation of GST exemption to shares set apart with respect to deceased children to such extent as property of which surviving spouse is transferor is insufficient to cause predeceased child exception to eliminate liability.	Elimination of vulnerability is more important for shares set apart with respect to deceased children than for shares set apart with respect to living children.	Predeceased child exception avoids generation-skipping transfer for shares set apart with respect to deceased children and does not apply to shares set apart with respect to living children. Subject to eliminating GST involvement for each share equally except to any extent that a benefit to one share does not produce a detriment to another, attempt to use (i) GST exemption (*i.e.*, allocate property of which each spouse is transferor, to extent of each's GST exemption) for shares set apart with respect to living children and (ii) predeceased child exception (*i.e.*, allocate property of which surviving spouse is transferor in excess of that to which GST exemption is allocable) for shares set apart with respect to deceased children.	Equal importance.
	Action and Drafting Solution (applicable only to **(1)**, *i.e.*, not **(2)**): First, if the division into shares occurs upon the death of the surviving spouse, allocate pro rata to each share that is set apart with respect to a deceased child property of which the surviving spouse is the transferor in excess of that to which GST exemption is allocable. Second, allocate exempt or exemptible property of which each spouse is the transferor pro rata to each share that is set apart with respect to a deceased child. Third, allocate any balance of the exempt or exemptible property pro rata to each share that is set apart with respect to a living child. See § 10.03, Form #D, *infra*.		**Action Solution** (same as Case B, applicable only to **(2)**, *i.e.*, not **(1)**): First, if the division into shares occurs upon the death of the surviving spouse, allocate pro rata to each share that is set apart with respect to a deceased child property of which the surviving spouse is the transferor in excess of that to which GST exemption is allocable. Second, allocate exempt or exemptible property of which each spouse is the transferor pro rata to each share that is set apart with respect to a living child, to the extent of the amount allocable to any share according to the preceding sentence. Third, allocate any remaining property pro rata to any balance of each share. See § 10.03, Form #C, *infra*. **Comment re Action Solution** (applicable only to **(2)**, *i.e.*, not **(1)**): This solution fails to take into account that the aging of the descendant before the allocation date (but after the execution of the instrument) might have transformed the disposition, before the allocation date, from a trust for ages into an outright disposition. This failure compounds as the number of shares (and the number of different ages of the descendants) increases. **Drafting Solution** Arguably, the drafting solution of choice is to mandate a tax result and, by implication, to mandate whatever allocation produces the tax result at the particular time. See § 10.03, Form #A, *infra*.	

	(1)		(2)	
	(a)	(b)	(a)	(b)
Case D (i) Trust for life; (ii) Outright	Predeceased child exception prevents generation-skipping transfer at, but not below, level of a child. Therefore, rely on predeceased child exception only to extent that GST exemption is insufficient.	Elimination of GST vulnerability is important *only* for shares set apart with respect to deceased children.	Predeceased child exception prevents generation-skipping transfer at, but not below, level of a child. Therefore, rely on predeceased child exception only to extent that GST exemption is insufficient.	Elimination of GST vulnerability is important *only* for shares set apart with respect to deceased children.

Action and Drafting Solution (applicable to **(1)** and **(2)**): First, allocate exempt or exemptible property of which each spouse is transferor pro rata to the shares that are set apart with respect to deceased children. Second, if the division into shares occurs upon the death of the surviving spouse, allocate other property of which the surviving spouse is the transferor pro rata to the shares that are set apart with respect to deceased children. See § 10.03, Form #E, *infra*.

	(1)		(2)	
	(a)	(b)	(a)	(b)
Case E (i) Trust for life; (ii) Trust for life	Predeceased child exception prevents generation-skipping transfer at, but not below, level of a child and, therefore, has some utility but low priority.	Equal importance. Shares set apart with respect to deceased children and with respect to living children are equally capable of producing generation-skipping transfers.	Predeceased child exception prevents generation-skipping transfer at, but not below, level of a child and, therefore, has some utility but low priority.	Equal importance. Shares set apart with respect to deceased children and with respect to living children are equally capable of producing generation-skipping transfers.

Action and Drafting Solution (applicable to **(1)** and **(2)**): First, allocate exempt or exemptible property of which each spouse is transferor pro rata to each share. Second, if the division into shares occurs upon the death of the surviving spouse, allocate other property of which the surviving spouse is the transferor pro rata to the shares that are set apart with respect to deceased children. See § 10.03, Form #F, *infra*.

	(1)		(2)	
	(a)	**(b)**	**(a)**	**(b)**
Case F (i) Trust for life; (ii) Trust for ages	Shares set apart with respect to living children are unlikely to produce any generation-skipping transfer. Predeceased child exception will not prevent generation-skipping transfer at level of grandchildren or below. Therefore, rely on predeceased child exception for shares set apart with respect to deceased children only to extent that GST exemption is insufficient.	Elimination of vulnerability is more important for shares set apart with respect to deceased children than for shares set apart with respect to living children.	Assumption is indulged that shares set apart with respect to living children are as likely to produce taxable terminations because of passage to grandchildren as shares set apart with respect to deceased children are likely to produce taxable terminations because of passage to great-grandchildren. Predeceased child exception will prevent generation-skipping transfer at, but not below, level of a child and, therefore, has some utility but low priority.	Equal importance.
	Action and Drafting Solution (same as Case D, applicable only to **(1)**, *i.e.*, not **(2)**): First, allocate exempt or exemptible property of which each spouse is transferor pro rata to the shares that are set apart with respect to deceased children. Second, if the division into shares occurs upon the death of the surviving spouse, allocate other property of which the surviving spouse is the transferor pro rata to the shares that are set apart with respect to deceased children. See § 10.03, Form #E, *infra*.		**Action Solution** (same as Case E, applicable only to **(2)**, *i.e.*, not **(1)**): First, allocate exempt or exemptible property of which each spouse is transferor pro rata to each share. Second, if the division into shares occurs upon the death of the surviving spouse, allocate other property of which surviving spouse is the transferor pro rata to the shares that are set apart with respect to deceased children. See § 10.03, Form #F, *infra*. **Comment re Action Solution** (applicable only to **(2)**, *i.e.*, not **(1)**): This solution fails to take into account that the aging of the descendant before the allocation date (but after the execution of the instrument) might have transformed the disposition, before the allocation date, from a trust for ages into an outright disposition. This failure compounds as the number of shares (and the number of different ages of the descendants) increases. **Drafting Solution**: Arguably, the drafting solution of choice is to mandate a tax result and, by implication, to mandate whatever allocation produces the tax result at the particular time. See § 10.03, Form #A, *infra*.	

	(1)		(2)	
	(a)	**(b)**	**(a)**	**(b)**
Case G (i) Trust for ages; (ii) Outright	Predeceased child exception prevents generation-skipping transfer at, but not below, level of a child. Therefore, rely on predeceased child exception only to extent that GST exemption is insufficient.	Elimination of GST vulnerability is important *only* for shares set apart with respect to deceased children.	Predeceased child exception prevents generation-skipping transfer at, but not below, level of a child. Therefore, rely on predeceased child exception only to extent that GST exemption is insufficient.	Elimination of GST vulnerability is important *only* for shares set apart with respect to deceased children.

Action Solution (same as Case D, applicable to **(1)** and **(2)**): First, allocate exempt or exemptible property of which each spouse is transferor pro rata to the shares that are set apart with respect to deceased children. Second, if the division into shares occurs upon the death of the surviving spouse, allocate other property of which the surviving spouse is the transferor pro rata to the shares that are set apart with respect to deceased children. See § 10.03, Form #E, *infra*.

Comment re Action Solution (applicable to **(1)** and **(2)**): This solution can take into account the tendency of a trust for ages to become an outright disposition as the descendant attains the required age(s) after the time as of which the property is allocated. However, it fails to take into account that the aging of the descendant before the allocation date (but after the execution of the instrument) might have transformed the disposition, before the allocation date, from a trust for ages into an outright disposition. This failure compounds as the number of shares (and the number of different ages of the descendants) increases.

Drafting Solution: Arguably, the drafting solution of choice is to mandate a tax result and, by implication, to mandate whatever allocation produces the tax result at the particular time. See § 10.03, Form #A, *infra*.

	(1) (a)	(1) (b)	(2) (a)	(2) (b)
Case H (i) Trust for ages; (ii) Trust for life	Shares set apart with respect to deceased children probably will pass outright to grandchildren and predeceased child exception probably will avoid all generation-skipping transfers with respect to them. Therefore, while it will not prevent a generation-skipping transfer at level of grandchildren or below, predeceased child exception has high utility.	Equal importance.	Assumption is indulged that shares set apart with respect to deceased children are as likely to produce taxable terminations because of passage to great-grandchildren as shares set apart with respect to living children are likely to produce taxable terminations because of passage to grandchildren. Predeceased child exception will prevent a generation-skipping transfer at, but not below, level of a child and, therefore, has some utility but low priority.	Equal importance.

Action and Drafting Solution (same as Case B, applicable only to **(1)**, *i.e.*, not **(2)**): First, if the division into shares occurs upon the death of the surviving spouse, allocate pro rata to each share that is set apart with respect to a deceased child property of which the surviving spouse is the transferor in excess of that to which GST exemption is allocable. Second, allocate exempt or exemptible property of which each spouse is the transferor pro rata to each share that is set apart with respect to a living child, to the extent of the amount allocable to any share according to the preceding sentence. Third, allocate any remaining property pro rata to any balance of each share. See § 10.03, Form #C, *infra.*

Comment re Drafting Solution (applicable only to **(1)**, *i.e.*, not **(2)**): Step Third requires pro rata allocation. This allocation seems possible without drafting.

Action Solution (same as Case E, applicable only to **(2)**, *i.e.*, not **(1)**): First, allocate exempt or exemptible property of which each spouse is transferor pro rata to each share. Second, if the division into shares occurs upon the death of the surviving spouse, allocate other property of which the surviving spouse is the transferor pro rata to the shares that are set apart with respect to deceased children. See § 10.03, Form #F, *infra.*

Comment re Action Solution (applicable only to **(2)**, *i.e.*, not **(1)**): This solution fails to take into account that the aging of the descendant before the allocation date (but after the execution of the instrument) might have transformed the disposition, before the allocation date, from a trust for ages into an outright disposition. This failure compounds as the number of shares (and the number of different ages of the descendants) increases.

Drafting Solution: Arguably, the drafting solution of choice is to mandate a tax result and, by implication, to mandate whatever allocation produces the tax result at the particular time. See § 10.03, Form #A, *infra.*

	(1)		(2)	
	(a)	(b)	(a)	(b)
Case I (i) Trust for ages; (ii) Trust for ages	Although child of deceased child probably is younger than living child and thus has greater chance of dying before attaining age(s) at which trust terminates, shares set apart with respect to deceased children probably will pass outright to grandchildren and shares set apart with respect to living children probably will pass outright to children. Probably, only shares set apart with respect to deceased children will produce any generation-skipping transfer. Probably, predeceased child exception will avoid all generation-skipping transfers.	Elimination of vulnerability is more important for shares set apart with respect to deceased children than for shares set apart with respect to living children.	Assumption is indulged that shares set apart with respect to deceased children are as likely to produce taxable terminations because of passage to great-grandchildren as shares set apart with respect to living children are likely to produce taxable terminations because of passage to grandchildren.	Equal importance.
	Action and Drafting Solution (same as Case A, applicable only to **(1)**, *i.e.*, not **(2)**): Allocate to the shares that are set apart with respect to deceased children property that is GST-exempt or exemptible or, if the division into shares occurs upon the death of the surviving spouse, (i) property that is GST-exempt or exemptible and (ii) other property of which the surviving spouse is the transferor. See § 10.03, Form #B, *infra*.		**Action Solution** (same as Case E, applicable only to **(2)**, *i.e.*, not **(1)**): First, allocate exempt or exemptible property of which each spouse is transferor pro rata to each share. Second, if the division into shares occurs upon the death of the surviving spouse, allocate other property of which the surviving spouse is the transferor pro rata to the shares that are set apart with respect to deceased children. See § 10.03, Form #F, *infra*. **Comment re Action Solution** (applicable only to **(2)**, *i.e.*, not **(1)**): This solution fails to take into account that the aging of the descendant before the allocation date (but after the execution of the instrument) might have transformed the disposition, before the allocation date, from a trust for ages into an outright disposition. This failure compounds as the number of shares (and the number of different ages of the descendants) increases. **Drafting Solution**: Arguably, the drafting solution of choice is to mandate a tax result and, by implication, to mandate whatever allocation produces the tax result at the particular time. See § 10.03, Form #A, *infra*.	

Case	(1) Summary of Action and Drafting Solutions Assuming that Actuarial Probability is Dominant Criterion		(2) Summary of Action and Drafting Solutions Assuming that Maintenance of Per Stirpital Allocation is Dominant Criterion	
	Action Form	**Drafting Form**	**Action Form**	**Drafting Form**
A (i) Outright; (ii) Outright	B	A or B	B	A or B
B (i) Outright; (ii) Trust for life	C	A or C	C	A or C
C (i) Outright; (ii) Trust for ages	D	A or D	C	A
D (i) Trust for life; (ii) Outright	E	A or E	E	A or E
E (i) Trust for life; (ii) Trust for life	F	A or F	F	A or F
F (i) Trust for life; (ii) Trust for ages	E	A or E	F	A
G (i) Trust for ages; (ii) Outright	E	A	E	A
H (i) Trust for ages; (ii) Trust for life	C	A or C	F	A
I (i) Trust for ages; (ii) Trust for ages	B	A or B	F	A

Assumptions:

1. Effective tax rates (*i.e.*, gift tax, estate tax, and generation-skipping tax (including on direct skips and taxable terminations)) are the same.
2. The time use of money has no value.

Observations:

When a trust for ages is used, the principal object is to benefit the income beneficiary but to provide management during immaturity. A trust for life, on the other hand, might signify an intent to benefit persons in more than one generation.

§ 10.03 TABLE I FORMS

Form #A

The Trustee shall allocate among the shares so set apart (i) property of which I am the transferor for generation-skipping tax purposes and (ii) property of which my [wife] [husband] is the transferor for generation-skipping tax purposes, in such equitable manner as, given this instrument but assuming no discretionary distribution or appointment, permits the transfer of the property with the least generation-skipping tax to my descendants, per stirpes, living from time to time

a [, determined, however, as if each right of a descendant to withdraw principal from a trust at all times after the creation of the right

ai [were exercisable at all times from and after]

aii [exists only if the right is exercisable at]

the time as of which the division into shares occurs].

---

a — Use if any share is in format of trust for ages.
ai — Use if actuarial probability is dominant criterion.
aii — Use if maintenance of per stirpital allocation is dominant criterion.

Form #B

To the extent other property is available for other shares, the Trustee shall allocate to each share so set apart with respect to a deceased child of mine only (I) property that has an inclusion ratio of zero (or would have an inclusion ratio of zero if (i) it were allocated pro rata to, and were the only asset of, each share so set apart with respect to a deceased child of mine and (ii) my GST exemption that is unallocated immediately before my death were allocated pro rata to it or my [wife's] [husband's] GST exemption that is unallocated immediately before my [wife's] [husband's] death, minus the amount of my [wife's] [husband's] GST exemption that, if allocated, would eliminate all liability for generation-skipping tax upon all transfers of all property of which my [wife] [husband] is the transferor for generation-skipping tax purposes and that does not pass according to this instrument, were allocated pro rata to it) and (II) if the division into shares occurs upon my death, other property of which I am (or, if the division into shares occurs upon the death of my [wife] [husband]

a [simultaneously with or]

after my death, my [wife] [husband] is) the transferor for generation-skipping tax purposes.

---

a – Use if this instrument creates marital disposition if spouses die simultaneously.

Form #C

If the division into shares occurs upon my death or upon the death of my [wife] [husband], the Trustee shall allocate pro rata to each share so set apart with respect to a deceased child of mine (to the extent of the share) property of which, if the division into shares occurs upon my death, I am (or, if the division occurs upon the death of my [wife] [husband]

a [simultaneously with or]

after my death, my [wife] [husband] is) the transferor for generation-skipping tax purposes and that exceeds that which would have an inclusion ratio of zero if (i) it were allocated pro rata to (and were the only asset of) each share so set apart with respect to a deceased child of mine and (ii) my GST exemption that is unallocated immediately before my death or my [wife's] [husband's] GST exemption that is unallocated immediately before my [wife's] [husband's] death, minus the amount of my [wife's] [husband's] GST exemption that, if allocated, would eliminate all liability for generation-skipping tax upon all transfers of all property of which my [wife] [husband] is the transferor for generation-skipping tax purposes and that does not pass according to this instrument, were allocated pro rata to it. The Trustee shall allocate pro rata to each share so set apart with respect to a living child of mine (to the extent of the lesser of (i) the share and (ii) the property that is allocable to any share according to the sentence that immediately precedes this sentence) property that has an inclusion ratio of zero (or would have an inclusion ratio of zero if (i) it were allocated pro rata to, and were the only asset of, each share so set apart with respect to a living child of mine and (ii) my GST exemption that is unallocated immediately before my death were allocated pro rata to it or my [wife's] [husband's] GST exemption that is unallocated immediately before my [wife's] [husband's] death, minus the amount of my [wife's] [husband's] GST exemption that, if allocated, would eliminate all liability for generation-skipping tax upon all transfers of all property of which my [wife] [husband] is the transferor for generation-skipping tax purposes and that does not pass according to this instrument, were allocated pro rata to it). The Trustee shall allocate pro rata to any balance of each share (after taking account of the two sentences that immediately precede this sentence) any property that is not specially allocated according to either of the two sentences that immediately precede this sentence.

---

a – Use if this instrument creates marital disposition if spouses die simultaneously.

Form #D

If the division into shares occurs upon my death or upon the death of my [wife] [husband], the Trustee shall allocate pro rata to each share so set apart with respect to a deceased child of mine (to the extent of the share) property of which, if the division into shares occurs upon my death, I am (or, if the division occurs upon the death of my [wife] [husband]

a [simultaneously with or]

after my death, my [wife] [husband] is) the transferor for generation-skipping tax purposes and that exceeds that which would have an inclusion ratio of zero if (i) it were allocated pro rata to (and were the only asset of) each share so set apart with respect to a deceased child of mine and (ii) my GST exemption that is unallocated immediately before my death or my [wife's] [husband's] GST exemption that is unallocated immediately before my [wife's] [husband's] death, minus the amount of my [wife's] [husband's] GST exemption that, if allocated, would eliminate all liability for generation-skipping tax upon all transfers of all property of which my [wife] [husband] is the transferor for generation skipping tax purposes and that does not pass according to this instrument, were allocated pro rata to it. The Trustee shall allocate pro rata to each share so set apart with respect to a deceased child of mine (to the extent of any balance of the share after taking account of the sentence that immediately precedes this sentence) property that has an inclusion ratio of zero (or would have an inclusion ratio of zero if (i) it were allocated pro rata to, and were the only asset of, each share so set apart with respect to a deceased child of mine and (ii) my GST exemption that is unallocated immediately before my death were allocated pro rata to it or my [wife's] [husband's] GST exemption that is unallocated immediately before my [wife's] [husband's] death, minus the amount of my [wife's] [husband's] GST exemption that, if allocated, would eliminate all liability for generation-skipping tax upon all transfers of all property of which my [wife] [husband] is the transferor for generation-skipping tax purposes and that does not pass according to this instrument, were allocated pro rata to it). The Trustee shall allocate pro rata to each share so set apart with respect to a living child of mine (to the extent of the share) any balance (after taking account of the sentence that immediately precedes this sentence) of the property described in the sentence that immediately precedes this sentence.

---

a – Use if this instrument creates marital disposition if spouses die simultaneously.

Form #E

The Trustee shall allocate pro rata to each share so set apart with respect to a deceased child of mine (to the extent of the share) property that has an inclusion ratio of zero (or would have an inclusion ratio of zero if (i) it were allocated pro rata to, and were the only asset of, each share so set apart with respect to a deceased child of mine and (ii) my GST exemption that is unallocated immediately before my death were allocated pro rata to it or my [wife's] [husband's] GST exemption that is unallocated immediately before my [wife's] [husband's] death, minus the amount of my [wife's] [husband's] GST exemption that, if allocated, would eliminate all liability for generation-skipping tax upon all transfers of all property of which my [wife] [husband] is the transferor for generation-skipping tax purposes and that does not pass according to this instrument, were allocated pro rata to it). If the division into shares occurs upon my death or upon the death of my [wife] [husband], the Trustee shall allocate pro rata to each share so set apart with respect to a deceased child of mine (to the extent of any balance of the share after taking account of the sentence that immediately precedes this sentence) any property of which, if the division into shares occurs upon my death, I am (or, if the division occurs upon the death of my [wife] [husband]

a [simultaneously with or]

after my death, my [wife] [husband] is) the transferor for generation-skipping tax purposes and which is not specially allocated according to the sentence that immediately precedes this sentence.

---

a – Use if this instrument creates marital disposition if spouses die simultaneously.

Form #F

The Trustee shall allocate pro rata to each share so set apart property that has an inclusion ratio of zero (or would have an inclusion ratio of zero if (i) it were allocated pro rata to, and were the only asset of, each share so set apart and (ii) my GST exemption that is unallocated immediately before my death were allocated pro rata to it or my [wife's] [husband's] GST exemption that is unallocated immediately before my [wife's] [husband's] death, minus the amount of my [wife's] [husband's] GST exemption that, if allocated, would eliminate all liability for generation-skipping tax upon all transfers of all property of which my [wife] [husband] is the transferor for generation-skipping tax purposes and that does not pass according to this instrument, were allocated pro rata to it). If the division into shares occurs upon my death or upon the death of my [wife] [husband], the Trustee shall allocate pro rata to each share so set apart with respect to a deceased child of mine (to the extent of any balance of the share after taking account of the sentence that immediately precedes this sentence) any property of which, if the division into shares occurs upon my death, I am (or, if the division occurs upon the death of my [wife] [husband], my [wife] [husband] is) the transferor for generation-skipping tax purposes and which is not specially allocated according to the sentence that immediately precedes this sentence.

11

Allocation of Property with GST-Significant Characteristics

§ 11.01 INTRODUCTION

This chapter is a comparison of two systems of allocation of property to, or for the benefit of, children and more remote descendants after the death of the surviving parent of the children. The comparison is intended to provide insights that can serve as a basis for drafting. Step-by-step procedures for "optimal handling" ("System I") and for "nonoptimal handling" ("System II") are outlined in §§ 11.02 and 11.03, *infra*. The advantages or disadvantages of each system are discussed in §11.04, *infra*. A factual example and accompanying "flow charts," which illustrate the operations of each of the systems, are presented in § 11.05, *infra*.

§ 11.02 OPTIMAL HANDLING ("SYSTEM I")

Channel all of the marital trust(s), all of the disclaimer trust, and all of the credit shelter trust into one receptacle — for example, "to the Trustee of the Family Trust." Do not specify in any originating trust that one type of property has one destination and another type of property has another or that the originating trust has a destination that is different from the destination of another originating trust. Specify the ultimate destinations only in the single receptacle (for example, the Family Trust) from which the ultimate dispositions are made. Use the single receptacle as a conduit through which to pass particular types of property to particular destinations.

Divide the receptacle (for example, the Family Trust) into a portion that is anticipated to be exempt (that is, "Portion 1") and a portion that is anticipated to be nonexempt (that is, "Portion 2").

Divide the receptacle (for example, the Family Trust) conceptually, not physically, into shares for descendants. The purpose of this division is to determine the size, not the character of the content, of each share. Accordingly, for purposes of making this division, assume that the Family Trust is not divided into Portions 1 and 2.

Allocate to the shares, pro rata or non-pro rata, as is appropriate for the dispositive formats: (i) Portion 1, (ii) the part of Portion 2 of which the predeceasing spouse is the transferor, and (iii) the part of Portion 2 of which the surviving spouse is the transferor.

Provide separately for the administration of Portion 1 of each share and for the administration of Portion 2 of each share.

§ 11.03 NONOPTIMAL HANDLING ("SYSTEM II")

Divide the property in the receptacle trust (for example, the Family Trust), or in each originating trust (that is, the marital trust(s), the disclaimer trust, and the credit shelter trust), into a portion that is anticipated to be exempt (that is, "Portion 1") and a portion that is anticipated to be nonexempt (that is, "Portion 2").

Divide Portion 1 into shares — that is, allocate it pro rata to each share.

Separately, divide Portion 2 into shares — that is, allocate it pro rata to each share.

Provide separately for the administration of Portion 1 of each share and for the administration of Portion 2 of each share.

§ 11.04 OBSERVATIONS

System I permits pro rata or non-pro rata allocation to the shares, as is appropriate for the dispositive formats, of property of each complexion.

System II, on the other hand, requires pro rata allocation of property of each complexion.

Specification in each of the originating trusts (that is, the marital trust(s), the disclaimer trust, and the credit shelter trust) that one type of property has one destination and another type of property has another, or that the originating trust has a destination which is different from the destination of another originating trust, tends to produce the effect of System II.

System I can allocate property of different transferors non-pro rata to shares for living children and shares for children of deceased children — that is, it permits the possibility of non-pro rata allocation of property with particular characteristics. Therefore, the coupling of (i) System I and (ii) a particular disposition of a descendant's share to the extent the share consists of property with one characteristic and a different disposition to the extent the share consists of property with another characteristic creates the possibility that the sequence of deaths of descendants will affect the character of the dispositions.

Arguably, the technique of channeling all property to a *single* receptacle and providing solely in that receptacle (rather than in each originating trust) for all allocations of the property is easier for a reader to understand and easier for a draftsperson to use. It permits the draftsperson and the reader to focus one time, in one place, upon all of the property. By marshalling all of the property in one place, it subjects the optimal portion of the property to non-pro rata allocation.

While the marshalling technique potentially is useful in any event, it is particularly important if (i) the governing instrument of a predeceased spouse does not allocate optimally and (ii) the surviving spouse is a donee of a power to appoint the property that is subject to the governing instrument of the predeceased spouse. The surviving spouse can exercise the power to channel the property to a single receptacle (for example, the Family Trust) that he or she can create according to a new governing instrument. The surviving spouse can use the receptacle (that is, the Family Trust) to marshall all of the property of which the predeceased spouse is the transferor and all of the property of which the surviving spouse is the transferor. By contrast, an exercise of his or her powers to allocate separately (i) the property that is subject to the predeceased spouse's governing instrument and (ii) the property that is subject only to the surviving spouse's governing instrument can subject less than the optimal portion of the property to non-pro rata allocation.

§ 11.05 A FACTUAL EXAMPLE

The governing instrument of a predeceased spouse created upon his or her death (i) a qualified terminable interest property trust ("Marital Trust Number 1") with a value of $400,000, (ii) a qualified terminable interest property trust ("Marital Trust Number 2") with a value of $1,000,000, and (iii) a credit shelter trust with a value of $600,000. See the accompanying "flow charts," "System I" and "System II," following the description in this § 11.05, **Figures 11.2** and **11.3.**

The credit shelter trust is fully exempt because the executor of the predeceased spouse allocated $600,000 of the GST exemption of the predeceased spouse to it.

Marital Trust Number 1 is fully exempt because the executor of the predeceased spouse made an election under Code Section 2652(a)(3) and allocated the remaining $400,000 of the GST exemption of the predeceased spouse to it.

The descendants of each spouse are the same. They consist of (i) a child who predeceased the surviving spouse, (ii) a child who survived the surviving spouse, and (iii) a grandchild who is a child of the predeceased child and who survived the surviving spouse.

Upon the death of the surviving spouse, the governing instrument of the predeceased spouse creates (i) for each living child, a trust for the life of the child, remainder outright to the child's descendants, and (ii) with respect to each deceased child, outright gifts to the descendants, per stirpes, of the child.

Upon the death of the surviving spouse (after payment of estate tax), Marital Trust Number 1 has a value of $400,000, Marital Trust Number 2 has a value of $2,000,000, and the credit shelter trust has a value of $600,000. The surviving spouse had no property of his or her own.

Marital Trust Number 1 is added to the credit shelter trust, thus making a single, wholly exempt trust with a value of $1,000,000.

The credit shelter trust, thus enhanced to $1,000,000, is allocated pro rata, $500,000 to the trust for the surviving child, and $500,000 to the child of the deceased child.

The trustee of Marital Trust Number 2 splits it into two trusts. The executor of the surviving spouse allocates the GST exemption of the surviving spouse to one of the two trusts into which Marital Trust Number 2 was split.

The trust that is exempt because the GST exemption of the surviving spouse is allocated to it is added to the credit shelter trust.

This exempt, $1,000,000 enhancement of the credit shelter trust is also allocated pro rata, $500,000 to the trust for the surviving child and $500,000 to the child of the deceased child.

The nonexempt trust of which the surviving spouse is the transferor also is allocated pro rata, $500,000 to the trust for the surviving child and $500,000 to the child of the deceased child.

Proper, and feasible, planning would allocate $1,500,000 of exempt property and no nonexempt property to the trust for the child and $500,000 of exempt property and $1,000,000 of nonexempt property to the child of the deceased child.

The described arrangement, on the other hand, would cause allocation of $500,000 of nonexempt property and only $1,000,000 of exempt property to the trust for the child (thereby causing the generation-skipping transfer upon the death of the child to generate liability for tax) and would cause allocation of $1,000,000 of exempt property and only $500,000 of nonexempt property to the child of the deceased child (thereby effectively causing a wasted use of $500,000 of GST exemption rather than a tax-saving use of $500,000 of predeceased child exception).

Figures 11.1, 11.2, and **11.3,** which follow, illustrate the operation of the systems.

Figure 11.1
Optimal and Nonoptimal Handling

	Optimal		Nonoptimal	
	Trust for child for life	*Outright to grandchild*	*Trust for child for life*	*Outright to grandchild*
a) Exempt	1,500,000	500,000	1,000,000	1,000,000
b) Nonexempt				
i) Predeceased spouse is transferor.	0	0	0	0
ii) Surviving spouse is transferor.	0	1,000,000	500,000	500,000
Total	1,500,000	1,500,000	1,500,000	1,500,000

* * *

Figure 11.2
System I
(Optimal)

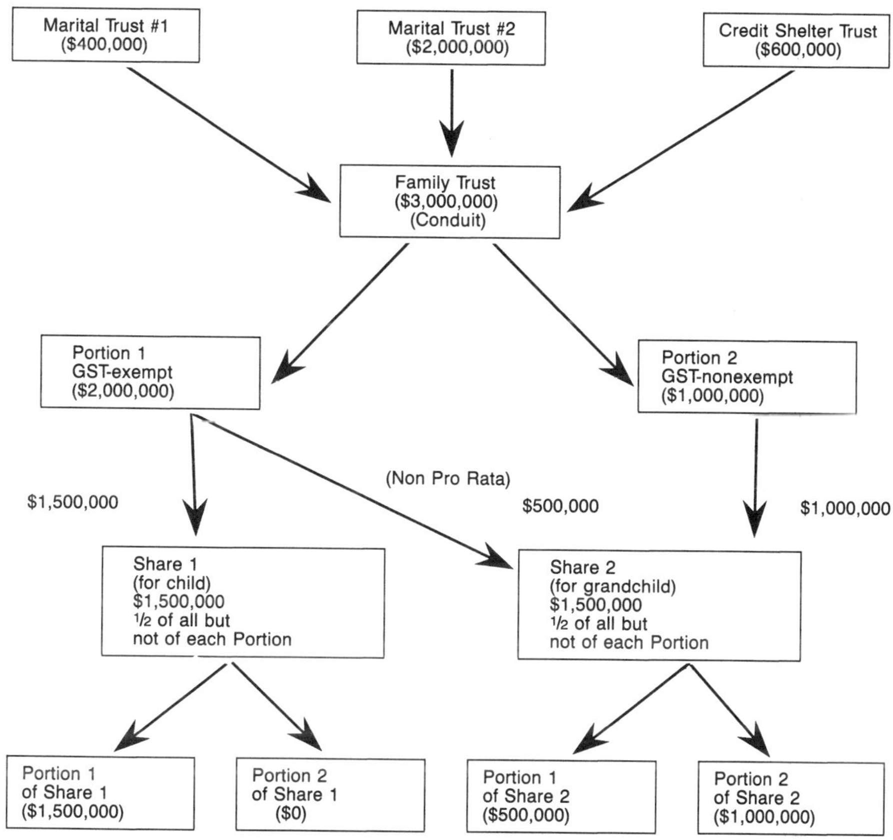

Figure 11.3
System II
(Nonoptimal)

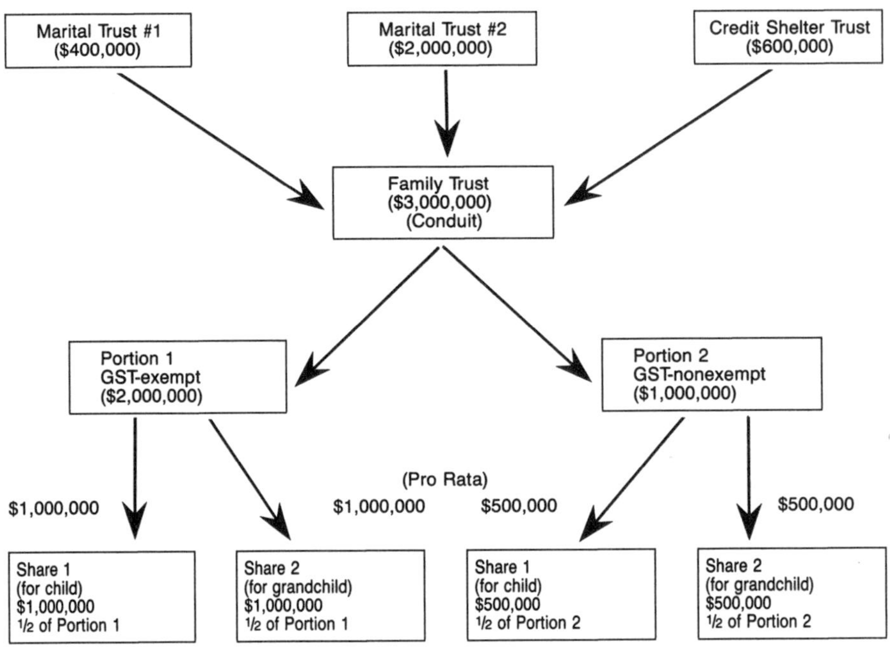

Appendix of Forms

The following forms, to which specific reference is made in the several tables in § 9.04, *supra,* and in other parts of this book, are included for discussion purposes only. Some of the forms are mere examples of procedures that generically are described in the text.

Form #1

(18) To divide, at any time (as of that or any earlier time), any trust (before or after it is funded) into separate trusts that consist of portions that at the actual time of division are, or (based on fair market values) have the economic effect of, fractional shares of the undivided trust, including, without limitation,

(i) portions that for United States generation-skipping tax purposes have (or, if GST exemption were allocated, would have) different inclusion ratios,

(ii) the portions, respectively, to which a power of appointment or withdrawal does, and does not (or, if the power were granted or, in the case of a testamentary power, the donee immediately were to die, or both, would, and would not) apply and

(iii) portions that for United States generation-skipping tax purposes have (or, if an election were made, would have) different transferors.

(19) To segregate and administer separately (including, without limitation, by means of a separate share, fund or trust), at any time (as of that or any earlier time), any property that is directed to be added to or disposed the same as other property but that is distinctive for United States tax purposes.

Form #2

(C) *Marital Trusts 1 and 2.* Notwithstanding the preceding portion of this Section:

(1) *Creation.* The Trustee as of my death shall set apart,

(a) in a separate trust to be known as "Marital Trust Number 1," such fractional share or all, if any, of the Marital Trust as has a numerator equal to the amount (if any) by which (i) my GST exemption unallocated immediately before my death exceeds (ii) the value (for purposes of determining the United States estate tax payable because of my death) of the trust estate (if any) of the Remainder Trust under *Section [A],* and a denominator equal to the value for such purposes of the trust estate of the Marital Trust, and,

(b) in a separate trust to be known as "Marital Trust Number 2," the balance of the Marital Trust.

(2) *Administration.* The Trustee shall administer Marital Trust Number 1 and Marital Trust Number 2 as if each, separately, were the Marital Trust; provided, the Trustee shall pay principal to my wife pursuant to subsection (A)(2) of this Section, and shall pay taxes pursuant to subsection (B) of this Section, solely from Marital Trust Number 2 until Marital Trust Number 2 is exhausted.

Form #3

(C) *Marital Trusts 1 and 2.* Notwithstanding the preceding portion of this Section:

(1) *Creation.* The Trustee as of my death shall set apart,

(a) in a separate trust to be known as "Marital Trust Number 1," such fractional share or all, if any, of the Marital Trust as has a numerator equal to the amount (if any) by which (i) my GST exemption unallocated immediately before my death exceeds (ii) the value (for purposes of determining the United States estate tax payable because of my death) of the trust estate (if any) of the

Remainder Trust under *Section [A],* and a denominator equal to the value for such purposes of the trust estate of the Marital Trust, and,

(b) in a separate trust to be known as "Marital Trust Number 2," the balance of the Marital Trust.

(2) *Administration.* The Trustee shall administer Marital Trust Number 1 and Marital Trust Number 2 as if each, separately, were the Marital Trust; provided,

(a) if my wife survives me by fifteen months, the Trustee additionally shall pay to my wife so much or all, if any, of the principal of Marital Trust Number 2 as my wife directs in writing at any time or from time to time; and

(b) the Trustee shall pay principal to my wife pursuant to subsection (A)(2) of this Section, and shall pay taxes pursuant to subsection (B) of this Section, solely from Marital Trust Number 2 until Marital Trust Number 2 is exhausted.

Form #4

Section [B]. Family Trust. The Trustee shall set apart, in a separate trust to be known as the "Family Trust" and to be administered as provided in this Section, a

a [pecuniary amount. The pecuniary amount shall be the amount (if any) of my GST exemption unallocated immediately before my death. For purposes of satisfying the pecuniary amount each item of property distributed in kind shall be valued at its fair market value as of its date of distribution.]

b [fractional share of the trust estate that remains after satisfaction of all dispositions and payments under prior provisions of this instrument. The numerator of the fraction shall be the amount (if any) of my GST exemption unallocated immediately before my death. The denominator of the fraction shall be the value (for purposes of determining the United States estate tax payable because of my death) of the trust estate that remains after satisfaction of all dispositions and payments under prior provisions of this instrument.]

Form #5

(13) To make equitable division or distribution in cash or in kind (including undivided interests), or partly in each, and in non-pro rata shares and amounts, without consent of any beneficiary.

Form #6

(same as Form #A; see § 10.03, *supra*)

The Trustee shall allocate among the shares so set apart (i) property of which I am the transferor for generation-skipping tax purposes and (ii) property of which my [wife] [husband] is the transferor for generation-skipping tax purposes, in such equitable manner as, given this instrument but assuming no discretionary distribution or appointment, permits the transfer of the property with the least generation-skipping tax to my descendants, per stirpes, living from time to time

a [, determined, however, as if each right of a descendant to withdraw principal from a trust at all times after the creation of the right

ai [were exercisable at all times from and after]

aii [existed only if the right is exercisable at]

the time as of which the division into shares occurs].

Form #7

; provided, the Trustee shall distribute the Appointive Portion to such one or more appointees, including the creditors and the estate and the creditors of the estate of the child, in such amounts and portions and subject to such trusts, terms and conditions as the child may appoint by Will specifically referring to

a [this power. The Independent Trustee at any time or from time to time may revoke or restore all or any of the power granted according to the provisory clause of the preceding sentence, as the Independent Trustee determines to be advisable,]

b [and in accordance with any power granted pursuant to the next sentence and in existence at the death of the child. Subject to the preceding sentence and except to such extent (if any) as the Independent Trustee has released this authority, the Independent Trustee at any time or from time to time may grant to the child such general power of appointment (as defined in Section 2041 of the Code), if any, to appoint the Appointive Portion as the Independent Trustee determines to be advisable, or revoke all or any of any power so created, in each case]

by means of a signed instrument delivered before the death of the child to the child or (if the child is legally incapacitated) a person described in subsection (F) of *Section [C]*. The Independent Trustee shall not have any responsibility for any exercise of, or any failure to exercise, any authority granted in the preceding sentence. The Appointive Portion is any of the trust with respect to which a generation-skipping transfer would occur upon the death of the child if the child did not possess any power of appointment.

Form #8

; provided, if (pursuant to *Section [D]* (18) or (19)) more than one trust is held for the child according to this subsection (B), this power to withdraw shall apply to the same amount of principal as if all of the trusts were one, but the principal to which the power applies shall coincide with each trust (to the extent of the lesser of the power and the trust) sequentially in descending order of inclusion ratios of the trusts for generation-skipping tax purposes.

Form #9

Section [E]. Charges and Taxes. The Trustee shall pay, from the trust estate (other than any property excluded from my gross estate for purposes of determining the United States estate tax payable because of my death) as an expense of administration, directly or to my personal representative, without apportionment or reimbursement: expenses of my last illness and funeral, costs of administration of property wherever situated passing under my Will or this instrument or otherwise, other proper charges against my estate and estate, inheritance, transfer, succession, legacy and similar taxes (including any generation-skipping tax imposed by Chapter 13 of the Code or otherwise on any direct skip not resulting from a disclaimer, but excluding all other generation-skipping tax, and any interest and penalty) payable because of my death. The Trustee shall pay preresiduary legacies and devises given by my Will, to such extent as the Trustee possesses the property given.

Form #10

Section [F]. Property Subject to Certain Power of Appointment. I am granted a power of appointment ("Power") at Section 3.03 of the Declaration of Trust of John S. Smith dated January 15, 1971. If any descendant of John S. Smith survives me, I exercise the Power by directing that, upon my death, all property subject to the Power shall be distributed to the Trustee of the Portion Three Family Trust created at Section 3.07 of my Declaration of Trust dated August 25, 1992; provided,

(A) Upon the death of the survivor of the descendants of John S. Smith, each trust that is not sooner terminated shall terminate with respect to the property subject to the Power (and its proceeds), and the trustee shall distribute that property to the estate of the survivor of the descendants of John S. Smith; and

(B) Each trust that is not sooner terminated shall terminate with respect to the property subject to the Power (and its proceeds) twenty-one years after the death of the last to die of the descendants of John S. Smith in being at the death of John S. Smith, and the trustee shall distribute that property to the members of the group that consists exclusively of the persons to whom, immediately before the termination, the trustee must or may pay income, in proportion to those interests or, to any extent indefinite, to the then-living descendants, per stirpes, of John S. Smith, determined as if each descendant who is not a member is deceased, or, if no member is a descendant of John S. Smith, to the members in equal shares.

Form #11

The Trustee shall make any payment to, or for the benefit of, a beneficiary from any trust that has more than one transferor for generation-skipping tax purposes (i) pro rata, from the separate portions attributable to transferors relative to whom the beneficiary is a non-skip person for generation-skipping tax purposes, and, to the extent of any balance, (ii) in ascending order of inclusion ratios of the portions for generation-skipping tax purposes, from the separate portions attributable to transferors relative to whom the beneficiary is a skip person for generation-skipping tax purposes.

Table of Cases

(References are to section numbers)

Table of Statutes, Rules, and Regulations

(References are to section numbers)

Internal Revenue Code of 1986

Internal Revenue Code of 1954

Tax Reform Act of 1986 (TRA '86)

Tax Reform Act of 1976 (TRA '76)

Treasury Regulations

Proposed Treasury Regulations

Revenue Procedures

Revenue Rulings

House of Representatives Report

Federal Register

Index of Subjects

(References are to section numbers)

F

G

Q

R

S

T

U

V

W